BETWEEN CLASSES
Faculty Life at Truman High

BETWEEN CLASSES
Faculty Life at Truman High

Charles E. Bruckerhoff

Teachers College, Columbia University
New York and London

To Viola Marie, Norbert, and Anna Rose

Published by Teachers College Press, 1234 Amsterdam Avenue
New York, NY 10027

Library of Congress Cataloging-in-Publication Data

Bruckerhoff, Charles.
    Between classes : faculty life at Truman High / Charles E.
Bruckerhoff.
       p.   cm
    Includes bibliographical references (p.) and index.
    ISBN 0-8077-3076-9 (alk. paper).—ISBN 0-8077-3075-0 (pbk. :
alk. paper)
    1. High school teachers—United States—Case studies. 2. High
school teaching—United States—Case studies. 3. High schools—
United States—Administration—Case studies.   I. Title.
LB1737.U6B75   1991
373.11'0092—dc20   90-21237

Printed on acid-free paper

Manufactured in the United States of America

98 97 96 95 94 93 92 91   8 7 6 5 4 3 2 1

Contents

Foreword *by Louis M. Smith*   vii

Preface   ix

1. Teachers in Their Workplace   1

2. The High School in Rillton   12
    Rillton, USA   14
    Truman High School   22
    The Social Studies Department   32
    Summary   35

3. The Cliques   37
    Academics and Coaches   38
    Playing Ball, Huddling, and Working the Shit Detail   43
    Black Humor, Playing the Game, and Pimping   51
    Summary   59

4. The Routine   61
    The Ride Home   63
    Lecture and Recitation   68
    Deadness Versus Vitality   73
    The Trap   76
    Summary   83

5. Escape   85
    Feeling Fresh   90
    Built-in Escapes   92
    Secret Escapes   94
    Summary   99

6. Benign Neglect   101
    Subject Matter   106

The Classroom   112
Gym and Professional Library   116
Summary   120

7. Between Today and Tomorrow   **123**

References   129

Index   133

About the Author   143

Foreword

Professional opportunities always come at particular times, occasions, and places in one's work life. When Charles asked me to write a brief foreword to his book I was pleased to do so, for we had had several long discussions about *Between Classes*, first at Egon Guba's Alternative Paradigms conference before AERA in the Spring of 1989 and second over a long lunch in St. Louis some months later. In between those discussions, I had read an earlier draft of the book and found the prose clear, the stories vivid, and the ideas stimulating. Now, when the phone call came I was in the midst of "curriculum planning," that is, I was working out a syllabus for a new course, "The Classroom as a Pedagogical System," and doing all the kinds of things Decker Walker described in his naturalistic model of curriculum development. I wondered what Bruckerhoff's book would teach me that I could teach my class. Not a bad criterion for focusing some introductory comments, so it seemed to me.

The book is based on an intensive field study of Truman High School. His overall problem lies in a naturalistic account of faculty life. The sub-issues, foreshadowed problems, are how teachers make teaching livable in the workplace, how they interrelate with each other and their administrators, their department heads and principals. He could show my students how a perceptive participant observer goes about the business of this kind of inquiry. The quotes are pithy, poignant, and provocative. No question exists that he has been at Truman High and that the faculty and he have something to say.

Life in the social science department is the basic story. Two factions exist, the Academics and the Coaches. The factions have a history and a culture. The informal social structure is writ large. And the split spills over into the community for the Coaches are locals and live in Rillton, the locale of the Truman School. The Academics do not; they carpool together to and from neighboring Idolville. School is over for them at 3:45 as they drive off together.

The Rillton community's desire for a blend of curricular and co-curricular is left, by them, at the front door of the Truman High. Implications spin off in multiple directions, as one might guess. The particulars may vary, but the dilemmas are general. My students, be they teachers, administrators, or interested citizens, or be they innovators or traditionalists, or be they cosmopolitans or locals need to confront these issues, think about them, and try to work out practical actions and procedures in their own settings as they educate children and adolescents in their own schools.

Bruckerhoff tends to stay with "experience-near" phrasing of the ideas, the teachers' own labels for experiences and ideas. That has a kind of charm. Without giving his game away, who can resist "huddling," "playing ball," "working the shit detail," "black humor," and "pimping" as labels for teacher activities. Or the more elaborate "escapes," like "mental health days," some built-in and some secret. Being a teacher in social studies at Truman High has more to do with cultures than with technology, more with personalities than with behavioral objectives. And those, too, are good issues for debate and discussion among my students.

In short, if ethnography is to provide mirrors for men and women to see how others live their lives and thereby contribute to one's own choices, and I believe ethnography should, Bruckerhoff has made a significant contribution for professional educators. His colleagues, my students, and you will be stimulated to considerable thought and discussion as each reads *Between Classes*.

Louis M. Smith

Preface

This book about teachers stems from personal experience with the job and from the heartfelt comments my colleagues gave me upon leaving the high school where we had worked together for several years. On a day in June at the end of a school year, I was heading off to graduate school, to begin work on a Ph.D. in education. They were heading to their classrooms to collect their belongings for a summer vacation and to brace themselves for another year of teaching.

Over the years we had watched many would-be teachers come and go. All the others had left teaching to become school administrators or to take up different occupations, such as accounting, business, farming, food service, insurance, real estate, retail sales, and so forth. Some left quietly, almost secretly. We learned of their departures late in August. Some left saying loudly that they were relieved to be going. "Finally" and "officially," they were getting out of teaching.

There was fear mixed with joy in the voices of these men and women at my farewell party. This peculiar combination of feelings made their wishes sound like warnings. "Don't forget about us," they said. They wrote the same message on their farewell cards. Some of them asked why I would leave the classroom teaching but stay in education. They wanted assurance that my work at the university level would contribute to their work at the secondary level. I promised not to forget. Later that day, when I finished checking in my keys at the principal's office, a colleague was waiting at the door to the outside. She said affectionately, and with a touch of bravado, "Get the hell out of here, Bruck!" Her lower lip was quivering, and there were tears in her eyes. We embraced and said good-bye.

I left high school teaching with a firm resolve to know why I left and what made it possible for other teachers to stay. It occurred to me that the best way to explore these questions would be to go back one day to a high school, to look carefully at what was going on, and to ask searching questions of the right people.

In the fifteen years that I have been involved with education, I have taught grammar, literature, history, math, and reading at elementary, secondary, or college levels in full- and part-time jobs. Throughout this time I have remained curious about the occupational requisites for teaching. Considering my present involvement with teacher certification and my continuing interest in the improvement of teaching, venturing into the schools from time to time strikes me as an occupational imperative.

Based on that interest and the promise I had made, I began a research project on the work of teachers in a large consolidated high school during the 1980–81 school year. My research on teaching in high school continues now at a number of schools in a metropolitan area. This book is a report of my earlier findings.

Between Classes offers a description of the pranks, exploits, and schemes engaged in regularly at work by the teachers in a social studies department at a place I call Truman High School. That the social studies department became the group to study was in part fortuitous—these people accepted me—and in part intentional. Social studies teachers are an especially good choice for inquiry into the work of teachers because the issues embedded in their subject matter are reflected in the social, psychological, and educational complex in a high school. They are unlike math and science teachers, who can focus on pure intellectual theory to the exclusion of social and psychological concerns. Nonetheless, all teachers must eventually confront the humanity of their subject matter and of teaching itself. At Truman, the complex nature of high school teaching was something with which everyone struggled in the teachers' lounge, hallways, and faculty meetings. For these reasons, the activities and relationships of the social studies teachers were perceived to be representative of Truman's teachers as a whole.

The teachers had divided themselves into two cliques, which I call Academics and Coaches, and within these small, informal groups the various individuals had helped create the particular playful or harmful routines that enabled them to cope with the exhaustion, frustration, and disappointment that were part of the job. The women teachers made up a very small subgroup (14 percent) within the social studies department. Of the total Truman High School faculty, women constituted 32 percent, a figure considerably lower than the national statistic of 48 percent female teachers in junior and senior high schools (Grant & Lind, 1979). Most of the women at Truman taught business, language arts, or home economics, and they constituted the majority in these departments. Although differences in activity attributable to gender may have been present at Truman, they were not evident to me.

I followed these teachers wherever they went—classroom, locker room, teachers' lounge, bar, home, and so on. The field notes reflect the honesty that can emerge when participant and observer meet each other face-to-face. I hope that my explanation for why these behaviors occur strikes the reader as convincing. Whether done as a practical joke or for protection, the informal coping strategies, such as "pimping" and "secret escapes," served an essential role in the work experiences of the social studies teachers and were due, at least in part, to the organization of the workday in a high school.

The heart of this book is the analysis of collegiality among teachers, some aspects of which contribute to educational interests while other aspects satisfy the personal interests of teachers at the expense of students, other teachers, or administrators. I shall argue that the perceptions and behaviors of teachers are to some extent responses to the troublesome expectations for their work role and that the organization of the school day militates against teaching and learning. I shall also consider the relationship between the formal organization of schooling and the informal behaviors of teachers. Those who have an interest in the evaluation of schools will find this account useful. It draws attention to one factor to consider (although seldom recognized) in the face of proposals for change: intentionally and unintentionally fostering cooperation or resistance within the faculty subculture. Finally, I shall suggest some implications for the teachers' day-to-day voluntary interaction, for the reorganization of the teacher's work day, and for the formal role of the schoolteacher.

This report is not only about teachers, but also for teachers. It intends to promote the best interests of teachers alongside their counterparts in other workplaces. The occupation of teaching is not so different from the other career choices that only certain kinds of people can make this work a lifelong commitment. This is true even though few other lines of work require an adult to devote so many hours to the attention of youngsters and also to impart some knowledge or skill to them.

But do these rudimentary distinctions call for a special kind of person? In other words, are the people who work as teachers so

different as human beings that only they can fulfill the formal role
of educator? This is quite possibly a misleading, if not a damaging,
belief. It places responsibility for the ills of teaching solely on the
people who do this work. It says nothing about the conditions of
their workplace. Teachers are like other workers in that they are
able to realize their greatest potential where the conditions are
most favorable for the accomplishment of their goals. A more
fitting distinction is that the professional conduct of teachers includes a penchant for helping others to learn and a repertoire of
refined knowledge and skill that comes from extensive training
and experience. These are the elements of teaching in schools that
are most effective, and they lie beyond the ken of people in other
occupations.

There are numerous stories about bright, enthusiastic be-
ginners who leave the classroom for a different career within
three to five years after receiving their state certification to teach.
Did these people finally see that they lacked the stamina that
would make them fit for teaching? What about the old-timers?
Why did they stay in teaching? What makes it possible for them to
continue with the classroom work for so many years? It is tempt-
ing to conclude that some people are fit for teaching and others are
unfit. George Bernard Shaw is often quoted by those who hold
teachers in disrepute: "Those who can, do; those who can't, teach."
This witty aphorism not only reflects some personal bias on the
part of Shaw, it is too simplistic a view of teaching. Indeed, as
George Counts (1952) clarified, that same great dramatist also
said, "He who can do, does; he who can think, teaches."

The occupations of people affect their behavior in curious ways.
For instance, a mechanic will look at things somewhat differently
from a painter, nurse, or lawyer. How does a teacher look at
things? What do teachers do on the job to make their work meaningful? What happens on the job that makes people want to stay in
teaching?

These questions are important today because there is much
argument about the reform of education. Already, some influential people and agencies are introducing new policies and practices for teaching and teacher-training institutions. If the circumstances of work for teachers are changed in a significant way, the
behaviors typical of teachers may also change in some way. However, to assure a positive direction for change, it is important to
know what features of the job are contributing to old behaviors
that are undesirable. School reform must establish a workday that

is personally and intellectually vibrant for teachers, supporting a school culture that is truly democratic and educational for everyone who comes there to learn.

I wanted to explore these questions with people who did the work of high school teachers. The book you are about to read is an attempt to express what the workplace mentality contributes to the occupation of teaching. It reports on the activity that was typical of social studies teachers at Truman High. My concern was to prepare the account of contemporary high school teachers so that the reader would encounter descriptions of work that would be recognized as that common to teachers and understand how this activity evolved within the teacher's world.

In this book I rely upon what a veteran teacher knows about the circumstances of work on a day-to-day basis in a high school. I argue that the improvement of teaching should include serious attention to the conditions of work for schoolteachers, because the detrimental organization of their workday clashes with prevailing notions about the school as a place for learning. I am also concerned with exposing the cultural process unfolding naturally among subgroups of teachers, recognizing the latent potential for positive and valuable contributions as well as for negative and deleterious results. Whatever the conditions for work, teachers must take responsibility for the occupational image they construct.

Generally speaking, high schools are gigantic physical structures that house a complex institution. The individual teacher who works there is part of a social organization that has evolved particular ways for each of the different groups—administrators, teachers, and students—to act so that schooling is done to the satisfaction of the general public. Beneath the network of formal titles and institutional operations lie the tacit dimensions of personal engagement and expression and social activity that create the peculiar quality of life in a school. Because this investigation of teachers was by intent and design what is known as natural history, the observations made were, in a sense, ordinary and commonplace. To say that they were commonplace, though, would not be the same as saying that they were familiar. Educational research needs to have facts about the social situation in the schools made more familiar. Observing and interpreting small-group activity within the teacher's world, making the teacher's work routines familiar, and subjecting the work community of teachers to scrutiny were the main objects of this research.

     This book should appeal especially to pre-service and in-service
teachers, because they are in a unique position to influence in an
ongoing, positive way the emergence of a new image for the career
schoolteacher. School administrators, teacher educators, and public policy officials should find that the book illustrates very well
what vexes them most—the galling discrepancies between planning and implementation. I hope that it encourages teachers and
administrators to discuss the circumstances of work at their
schools. The results of continuous, honest, and deliberate inquiry
could lead to better, more respectful relations between the different groups who operate school programs and to more productive,
collaborative work among educators.
     Chapter 1 introduces the problems associated with working in
a high school and explains the conceptual framework I used for
this research. Chapter 2 describes the setting. Truman High
School is a pseudonym for a real school located in Rillton, a ficti-
tiously named town in the heartland of the United States. The
emphasis here is to familiarize the reader with important aspects
of life in the school and the community. In Chapter 3 the reader
meets the two cliques making up the social studies department.
The names I have given to the cliques, Academics and Coaches,
help to signify their distinctive characteristics. These informal,
small groups met on a voluntary basis between classes, during
lunch or preparation time, and after work. The teachers had
invented a variety of coping strategies, such as *huddling* and
pimping, that proved one's acceptance or status and contributed to
permanence of the cliques.
     Chapter 4 examines the actual teaching routines, such as lec-
ture and recitation, and shows the teachers' use of these routines
for avoiding common and, at times, inappropriate pitfalls on the
job. Chapter 5 discloses the attempts of teachers to rescue themselves from boring or unbearable circumstances at work. Built-in
escapes were readily available means for getting relief. Secret
escapes were desperate measures. Despite the prospect of being
put on intensive supervision, non-renewal, or fired by an administrator, teachers regularly took these risks. Chapter 6 considers the
effect of the teachers' workplace mentality on the curriculum, the
students, and the teachers themselves. The conditions of work and
the teachers' behaviors contributed to an institutional effect that I
call benign neglect. I have chosen a style of writing for the description and analysis of data that I hope will permit the reader to
explore and interpret the implications of these results for the

improvement of the teacher's work life. In the last chapter I consider the implications of these findings for the occupation of teaching. The discussion closes with some reflections on possible changes among teachers and the institution in which they serve.

If recent experience serves me well, the results will make pre-service teachers more alert to the issues of career exemplars and job socialization. It will strike veteran teachers as both real and familiar. During the years since conducting the research, I have reported many of the findings while teaching courses at the university. The readings in class never failed to make the experienced schoolteachers laugh or shake their heads in agreement. Sometimes we held long discussions about cliques of teachers at their schools and how the cliques carried on with activities similar to those at Truman. Teachers were always anxious to tell how it was at their schools. If anything was telling in their comments, it was a genuine desire as well as a readiness to change their image.

Throughout the years of writing, it was my good fortune to meet people who genuinely became interested in the book. Although I cannot acknowledge all of my debts, I do want to thank some friends and colleagues who have given me the benefit of their sincere commentary and encouragement. Above all I want to thank Herbert Kliebard. He encouraged me to inquire—to take a fresh look at teaching—when it was fashionable for graduate advisors to direct students in narrow and self-serving interests. His power of perception is remarkable. His loyalty to principles is humbling. Over the years, the conversations we shared have become consoling and inspiring memories. Herb is the mentor and friend who gave both inspiration and opportunity.

To the men and women of Truman High School, I express my sincerest gratitude for their honesty and willingness to let me into their work lives. In the early stages of the research, timely and sound advice came from Wayne Otto and Gary Wehlage. They also reminded me in personal ways that a good sense of humor was an essential aspect of writing. Donna Schleicher gave support and advice as a dear friend. I also am very grateful to a number of people for their friendship and critical commentary on the manuscript. For those gifts I would like to thank Susan Adler, Becky Carlson, Peggy Cohen, Bill Doll, Chip Edelsberg, Roger Eldridge, Terri Fredericka, Allan Glatthorn, Paula Goll, John and Mary Krogness, Bill Pinar, Ernie Schuttenberg, Phil Smith, and Dan Stannard. Dave Chatfield and Greg Mangino are computer experts who deserve special recognition for their wizardry.

In the final stages of writing, several people volunteered to read the manuscript. I cannot overestimate my appreciation for their close study. I am deeply grateful to Susan Barr, Eric Bredo, Joan Di Dio, and Louis Smith. They are schoolteachers and professors; the best of colleagues—the best teachers. I also want to express my thanks to Sarah Biondello and Ron Galbraith, the editors at Teachers College Press. From the prospectus stage onward, they believed in this project and helped make it into a book.

Finally, after all these years, I am humbled by the personal sacrifices made by my family. My sons, Jeffrey, Aaron, and Matthew, never complained and always returned affection. My wife, Theresa, is an inspiring teacher and knows the book firsthand. She is the best of critics and a most patient and loving friend.

CHAPTER 1

Teachers in Their Workplace

On most days between September and May, some 13 million youngsters in this country attend public high schools. Going through the doors each day with them are about 980,000 high school teachers. Aside from having a low opinion about the quality of education and a definite aversion to the occupation itself, many adults in the United States know little else about the work done by these men and women. The school is seen principally as a place of learning for young people. But it is also a place of work for adults.

The circumstances of work affect the lives of people. In every workplace men and women form informal associations that help to sustain them while on the job. The patterns of activity evolved by these small groups not only tell whether or not workers enjoy what they are doing but also indicate the kind of work structures that are more likely to support high levels of job satisfaction (see Kanter, 1977).

Increasing numbers of people are expressing concern about the quality of work and the quality of experience in the workplace. After canvassing workers in a wide variety of occupations, Studs Terkel (1974) made this observation: "Possibilities of another way, discerned by only a few before, are thought of—if only for a brief moment, in the haze of idle conjecture—by many today" (p. xiii). People in this country want to do work that is meaningful to them. "The work of teachers is central to everyone's concern," according to Ernest Boyer (1983), for "excellence in education is linked to economic recovery and to jobs. We're being told that better schools will move the nation forward in the high-tech race" (p. 5). Because teaching is an occupation that serves people—namely, youth— directly, the public high school should be perceived first of all as a place of work for people.

1

What does the occupation of teaching do to the people who enter it? Like men and women in other occupations, teachers struggle to get through the tedium of their workday. A list of tedious chores may include keeping attendance, filing reports, writing lesson plans, disciplining students, training for specific skills, leading discussion groups, delivering lectures, monitoring hallways and lavatories, serving as study hall proctor, grading papers, and correcting exams. A feature common to all is that a teacher does them over and over again in the same way, with the same subject matter, and with the same students (see Cusick, 1973; Sizer, 1985). Tedium rises out of routine and has ramifications for all involved.

Isolation is a particular feature of teaching that stems from the predominant work structure defined for teachers and has deep historical and literary roots (see Eggleston, 1892; Lortie, 1975; Maeroff, 1988; Sizer, 1985; Waller, 1932). High school teachers, for example, experience social isolation while on the job. There is little or no opportunity for collaborative work because a high school teacher has very little time in the day to interact with peers. Isolation from peers may lead to ineptness at fostering collegial relations with them. Constant involvement with adolescents for purposes of classroom instruction contributes in important ways to a teacher's perception of work, attitude toward the job, and selection of materials and activities for teaching. Sustained and recurrent association with high school students may cause a teacher to adopt patterns of activity appropriate for dealing with adolescents but inappropriate for relating to other adults.

These points about teaching in the high school raise some serious questions. The first question is, What aspects of the teacher's activity are attributable to the structure of work at school? Routines that are more or less typical of a teacher's workday, such as the rotation of classes, timing of assignments and exams, and methods of teaching, influence some of the high school teacher's activity. The type of authority that the school board, central office administrators, and building principal exercise will have an effect on the teacher's activities and beliefs. The mannerisms, antics, and emotional responses that are typical of the adolescents with whom teachers spend so much of their time will influence the activity of teachers at work. How do teachers conduct themselves in the classrooms and hallways of the school? The informal activity of teachers—between classes—provides a fertile medium for describing and explaining the conduct of teachers while on the job.

A second issue of concern is, How and why do particular workplace mentalities arise? The attitudes and beliefs characteristic of a group of teachers in one school might be different from those that prevail in another school. For instance, in one school teachers might be enthusiastic about their educational program, heavily involved in decision making, and eager to participate in co-curricular activities. In another school one might find a low level of morale, little or no involvement in curriculum planning, and strict adherence to the stipulations of a union contract. Such significant attitudinal differences may also exist in different departments within the same building (see Pallas, 1988). Most teachers would prefer to work with the high-morale group. However, these same teachers could evolve a different, counterproductive system of beliefs and habitual modes of conduct within the same school (see Cooper, 1988).

Realizing that varieties of responses are possible for a group of teachers in a particular situation, it makes sense to ask, Why do they act in this way and not in some other way? This third question is especially important where the activity of teachers tends not to support their prior concern for high performance in teaching and learning. It is simplistic to attribute these negative results to a lack of leadership from the principal or to claim that the teachers' union promotes laziness and protectionism.

If one decides, instead, to look long and carefully at a group of teachers in a particular setting, eventually it should be possible to identify various aspects of a workplace mentality and understand how they produce certain behaviors peculiar to a particular group of teachers. Such an investigation should be in sympathy with the circumstances of teachers, but it should also maintain a perspective that encourages a critical analysis of the cultural process and its results. In the end there should be a contribution to the reform of education. An investigation of this kind could argue more convincingly for reform that respects the nature of teaching and addresses the origins of both good and poor qualities in the conduct of teaching.

In great part, this book focuses on the *informal activity* of teachers who were on the faculty of the social studies department at Truman High School. The teachers' informal activity involved nonteaching events, such as visiting with colleagues, exercising, and riding to and from work. Formal activity consisted of work that is normally expected of teachers, such as applying teaching methods and disciplining students. I also explore the *sources* of the teachers' informal behaviors and perceptions. The two cliques formed by the teachers in the social studies department had voluntary membership and separate and competing belief systems. These cliques, which I call Academics and Coaches, were important because membership meant that teachers gained experience with and support for activities that helped them cope with aspects of work that they perceived as frustrating or unsatisfying.

The sources of the teachers' dissatisfaction with work were the formal organizational structure, including a top-down authority model, the wide variations in achievement and motivation among the adolescent students, and the divisive preferences among the teachers themselves for academic study (the Academics) or co-curricular activities (the Coaches). To some extent these features are common to the American high school. The response of the social studies teachers at Truman High School was to create two distinct subcultures that sustained them on the job but frequently led them to sacrifice educational aims for immediate and self-serving objectives.

In this book I express a concern with the relationship between the *workplace mentality* and the *conduct of teaching*. By "workplace mentality" I mean the belief systems, including knowledge, skills, and perceptions, that the teachers had evolved through social interaction in their small, primary groups. By "conduct of teaching" I am referring to the routines of activity actually engaged in by teachers while on the job. The behaviors that arose from the teachers' workplace mentality were useful for successfully completing the requirements for work and for effectively coping with the situation. Collegiality among these teachers engendered a workplace mentality peculiarly suited to the school where they worked. Their perceptions of work and what they did with and to one another, particularly during the short intervals of time between classes, is all part of what I call the *teacher's world*.

In general, the kinds of activity that these teachers engaged in go on wherever people get together for work or play. Teachers are not alone in their development of informal behaviors for support or relief. A common name for this activity is "horseplay." Frederick Taylor (1972), the "father of time study," called it "systematic soldiering" (p. 32) and devised time and motion studies to rid the workplace of non-productive worker activities. Taylor's mistake was in assuming that all informal socializing of workers on the job is against the best interests of business or industry. He viewed the work of laborers as a troublesome but necessary extension of the industrial machine. Managers might enjoy work as a human enterprise, but not the people needed to manipulate objects on the shop floor or the assembly line.

In Truman High School the informal behaviors of teachers not only relieved them of some kinds of stress or frustration associated with the job of teaching but also provided a social framework within which a teacher received encouragement from peers to join a group in some activity. The invitation to participate in informal activities was an indication of acceptance by and support from *the* significant small group in a teacher's adult social life at the school. However, some of the activities that Truman's teachers engaged in, such as *huddling*, supported the aims of the institution, while others, such as *pimping*, eroded the teachers' chances of accomplishing the good for which the school existed.

The social studies teachers had evolved a subculture devoted to resistance—a resistance that not only affected, but also assured the continuance of, competing interests within their own ranks and against the school authorities. The behaviors described here indicate the character of this resistance and show its negative influence on the educational program in the social studies department. The teachers could have recognized the peculiar circumstance that they faced and developed strategies that helped all to cope with the different and, at times, conflicting demands, while at the same time laying the groundwork for a better practice of teaching and a better formal organization for the high school. They did not, however, choosing instead to focus on petty interests, an informal policy that led to a continuation of the strife so characteristic of their intergroup collegial relations and teaching activities.

An important source for interpreting teacher conduct proved to be *unselfconscious teacher mannerisms*, the stereotypical responses that the teachers relied upon for dealing with various aspects of their work. For example, one evening during the fieldwork I was invited by Anthony Finley to accompany him to his house after work. His wife greeted both of us at the door and began to show me around their newly remodeled kitchen and dining room. As she was talking, her husband repeatedly interrupted and corrected her statements. I noticed that she was becoming annoyed at his conduct. When she had finally had enough of his interference, she turned to him saying sharply, "Stop being *teachy!*" The teacher immediately recognized that his conduct was inappropriate. His wife's remarks let him know that he was no longer in his classroom dealing in his usual way with the teenagers or his colleagues. This was a gathering of adults, and self-conscious adults do not act pedantically toward one another.

I use the expression *unselfconscious teacher mannerism* to signify the unreflective, stereotypical activity of teachers. The teacher in the above example was acting in a predisposed manner toward his wife and his guest. I had noticed similar conduct previously in the other teachers' treatment of students, administrators, and colleagues. Unselfconscious teacher mannerism proved to be a useful descriptor for a broad range of routine behavior which might otherwise be called didactic, affected, or pedantic.

The display of a particular mannerism may indicate that a person is a member of a particular occupational group (see Homans, 1950; Weber, 1947). Teachers, like other workers, have evolved their own variety of mannerisms. For example, that action stands out as a teacher's mannerism when someone purposefully corrects another person's grammar at a party of adults. Another example is the *teacher look*, a manner of expressing disapproval which, when given well, can cause another adult to stop talking, in the cramped quarters of an elevator or across the expanse of a meeting room. Such behaviors—to which category we must add the tendency to lecture on every topic—are overused routines of teaching. When teachers use these routines unselfconsciously, whether on or off the job, they may suffer from an occupational hazard of teaching.

Though perhaps eccentric, unselfconscious teacher mannerisms still may serve an educational purpose in the classroom; on the other hand, they can also be merely bad practice or lead to bad practice—activity on the job that is unacceptable to supervisors or beneath the dignity of teachers who have serious concerns about improving the occupation. Sometimes the unsuitable practice is done self-consciously. For example, it is bad practice for a teacher to embarrass students, causing them to experience emotional distress. Other examples of bad practice among teachers (at times self-conscious and other times unselfconscious) include writing phoney lesson plans, holding a poor attitude toward a subject, presenting a lesson in a careless manner, or acting in such a way as to cause physical, sexual, or psychological harm to students. The teacher in question may intend to do good for students, but the uncritical application of the particular classroom strategy may nonetheless lead to harm or miseducation. The resulting teaching activity might be considered adolescent, unrefined, or vulgar.

I use the workplace mentality at Truman High School to talk about the conduct of teaching. The department chairpersons, building principal, and district superintendent used the words *professional* or *unprofessional* to evaluate the character and effect of a teacher's actions on the job. In the best of circumstances these popular terms imply an ethic of service (Bell, 1976), but their positive result in practice depends upon an appropriate definition and policy (see Judge, 1988; Popkewitz, 1984; Vidich & Lyman, 1985). Also, I am focusing on what I see as crucial for professional conduct by the individual teacher, rather than that which makes one or another occupation a *profession*.

Professional conduct among teachers entails striving for the best application of routine teaching procedures and the ingenious spotting and solving of problems in order to promote learning among students. Professional conduct of teachers involves the positive self-conscious and unselfconscious use of what John Dewey called *reflective thinking*. The following quotation from Dewey's *How We Think* is perhaps his clearest and most concise definition of this term:

> *Active, persistent, and careful consideration of any belief or supposed form of knowledge in the light of the grounds that support it and the further conclusions to which it tends* constitutes reflective thinking. . . . [I]t includes a conscious and voluntary effort to establish belief upon a firm basis of evidence and rationality. (1909/1933, p. 9)

As the manifest result of reflective thought, professional conduct entails immediate, tactful action as well as decisions made as a consequence of prolonged and thoughtful deliberation (Dewey, 1929). In every instance where the practice of teaching is concerned, professional conduct serves educational aims.

An attempt to define the conduct of teachers also needs to encompass careless activity and reflective thought in the service of unprofessional effects. As Argyris and Schön (1974) argue, a practitioner eventually will face the choice to act or not to act responsibly because "conflicts are endemic to professional practice; their resolution demands personal commitment" (p. 163). Looked at on the positive side, the inevitability of crisis, such as a parent's complaint or a lawsuit, leads professional workers to reform their practice and points out the moral dimension of their work. In the words of Hillary Putnam (1989):

[O]ur capacity for exercising this virtue [choosing to think] is the
most significant moral capacity we have; it includes the claim that
a human being who has chosen not to think for himself about how
to live, or has been coerced or "conditioned" into being unable to
think for himself about how to live, has failed to live a fully human
life. (p. 62)

The negative result of reflective thought stems from an individual's choice, for whatever reason—including negligence and oper-
ant conditioning—not to take a stand that is appropriate and
reasonable. Whether done willfully or unwittingly, in the least it
obstructs one's full potential to be a person and ultimately inter-
feres with the pursuit of reasonable aims by some larger social
organization, such as a school.

Unprofessional conduct is the ill-advised or poor application of
routine teaching procedures and the systematic avoidance of problem solving in relation to concerns for positive results in teaching
and learning. The unprofessional conduct of teachers also involves
the use of reflective thinking, but for negative results. In one
instance the teachers may not care what results follow. In another
instance they may passively or overtly resist efforts intended to
improve their practice. At another time they may choose to do
something that deters achievement of educational aims.

In order to clarify the path and the obstacles that teachers face
in their pursuit of status as skilled craftspersons or professionals,
it helps to distinguish between routine activities whose application
is *self-conscious* or *unselfconscious* and whose results are either
suitable or *unsuitable* for teaching. The self-conscious decision on
the part of a teacher to engage in activity that is suitable for
teaching suggests that there is an operational definition of teaching that is consistent with the aims of education and is therefore
professional. The suitable, unselfconscious performance of a
teaching routine also has its place in the professional conduct of
teachers. In these instances the teacher's activity should flow as a
well-rehearsed routine—a benefit from reflective practice conducted prior to the event. The expressive arts, such as ballet,
illustrate well that it is inappropriate at times to stop and think
about one's performance. However, the teacher's use of unsuitable
activity, either self-conscious or unselfconscious, subverts the aims
of the school and perpetuates long-standing beliefs about disrepute among teachers (cf. Waller, 1932). The result is unprofessional conduct. Suitable and unsuitable teacher activities are mu-

tually exclusive, yet they often coexist in schools. The persistence of unsuitable teaching activities suggests one of two things: either there is a mischievous notion about teaching at work or a misconception exists about the idea of teaching and its influence on one's practice in the classroom.

Whatever the source of the problem, this naturalistic inquiry into teaching benefited from use of the following conceptual framework—the lens I use to describe and explain what transpired in the field. The practice of teaching is problematic because it is both a product of the individual teacher's reflective thinking and a benefit of this teacher's participation in a small, primary group. Each part makes an important contribution to both the idea and the practice of teaching. The idea can both lead action and follow action. Teachers who work in a particular place, at a particular time, hold in common a generalized idea about the practice of teaching. I call this the workplace mentality. Teachers will construct their idea of work within small groups over time through contributions from different individuals, each of whom has in mind a personal idea of work that more or less complements the more abstract, generalized idea.

There is a pragmatic relationship between the idea and the practice of teaching. When a person becomes a teacher, he or she has in mind an idea, however simple or complex and whether accurate or inaccurate, about how to be a teacher. George Herbert Mead (1938) called this kind of idea a *role expectancy*. The role expectation for teaching is the socially constructed, generalized idea of work that guides (not rules) the teacher's conduct for *formal* and *informal* aspects of the occupation. The formal aspect of the teacher's role includes an idea about one's conduct in routine duties, such as lecturing, monitoring hallways, and attending faculty meetings. The informal aspect of the teacher's role includes an idea about conducting oneself in such activities as engaging in small talk between classes, lunchroom banter, and dancing or a game of pool with colleagues after work. Both formal and informal functions are essential aspects of the teacher's job. The individual teacher's personal knowledge and history of participation in a particular small group influence the whole complex of the teacher role expectation.

The actual performance of a daily teaching activity coincides generally with the idea that a teacher has in mind about a formal or informal aspect of her or his role. There is a reciprocal, mutually beneficent or maleficent relationship between the ideas about formal and informal functions and the teacher's performance of specific routines. The relationship is maleficent when theory and practice inform each other in detrimental ways. For instance, maladaptive theory can be substantiated by uncritical action. During a performance the individual teacher may or may not be aware of the extent to which there is conflict or complementarity between the operating idea of teaching and its result in practice. In other words, there are times when teachers do something very well, such as providing an example to illustrate a point during a lecture, but at the time they are not thinking about what they are doing. They are simply performing the activity of lecturing, an unselfconscious teacher routine. By the same token, a teacher may be unaware that he or she is using an unsuitable technique for teaching. However, the anticipation of using some routine, or some portion of it, affords the teacher the opportunity to engage in reflective thinking about the performance; this in turn leads to a personal judgment as to whether the activity chosen or performed is suitable or unsuitable for the demands of the task (Schön, 1983). Experienced colleagues, supervisors, and students are also able to spot a teacher's activity that complements or fails to measure up to the generalized idea.

While the practice of teaching is, essentially, an individual effort, there is nothing deterministic about the enterprise. Over time, the practice of teaching evolves in response to circumstances existing in an individual school, accounting for changes in both the guiding ideas that teachers have about their practice and changes in the particular elements of practice (see Rorty, 1989). This is the most potent aspect of the concept. The ideas about teaching and the conduct of teaching in the classroom are verifiable forms of human conduct whose origins one can trace, within reason, to the personal decisions of individual teachers and to the ethos of their small groups. The collegial relations of teachers offer expressive details for interpreting the quality of the guiding ideas and their use in the practice of teaching. On the face of it, one may expect to find either professional or unprofessional conduct. However, if the conditions of work are suitable, then the men and women who teach may achieve a definition of practice that is the envy of any other occupational group.

This book attempts to improve teaching by drawing attention to teachers' self-conscious and unselfconscious behaviors that are unsuitable for the job. It looks at the collective, informal conduct of teachers that insiders (i.e., teachers and administrators) and outsiders (i.e., parents, students, and the general public) may view with regret or disapproval. Informal group behaviors will arise wherever people work together and have great potential for making the worklife bearable and meaningful. When workers' informal behavior disregards or contradicts an *ideal role expectation*, those behaviors contribute to a negative workplace mentality.

In addition, serious adults in other occupations will not tolerate for long formal or informal peer behavior that diverges significantly from role expectations; such behavior leads to low public opinion about the occupation generally and/or to loss of work opportunities for specific individuals. The workplace mentality of the social studies teachers at Truman High lent support to the public's view of teachers as second-rate, as men and women who are somehow not properly suited to the rigorous standards maintained for those who take up other occupations (cf. Wirth, 1979).

I am concerned with collegial relations that make life bearable and interesting for educators and lead to improvements in the policy and practice of schooling. An organization like a public high school is likely to have worthy aims. It should have a structure of work that respects the people who engage in the activities associated with teaching and learning. This high school should also encourage the participation of all in the continual advancement of better forms of work to help achieve the aims of the school (see Bluestone, 1989; Lieberman, Saxl, & Miles, 1988; Raywid, 1989; Wirth, 1989). However, when there are serious inconsistencies between the stated aims of the school and the policies designed to accomplish those aims, some of the people who must do the work will allow unreflective and unprofessional behaviors to typify conduct on the job.

The workplace mentality that is endemic to a subgroup of teachers is a critical feature of the school curriculum in that the everyday activities it fosters may support or detract from the educational interests of the school. Any effort to change the organization of work for teachers or to influence in some way the subculture of teachers must respect the precarious nature of this informal group activity. The small, informal group plays an important role in the occupation of teaching for both the individual members and for the larger, formal organization of the school. The conduct of teachers indicates the extent to which aims and policies of the school show respect or disregard for educational interests.

CHAPTER 2

The High School in Rillton

On a sunny, spring day I was in a downtown café having lunch with a teacher. We had just met at an education conference. For some time I had been talking with teachers about their work and was glad on that day to find another veteran teacher who had something to say about the job. We talked for the rest of that afternoon about education, particularly about the conduct of teaching in high school.

His description of the situation where he worked became more and more interesting the longer I listened. He loved to teach, he said, but there was so much that stood in the way, especially the "other teachers and the damn administrators." I had heard that phrase before, and it struck me then as an important clue to unraveling some of the mystery surrounding this occupation. At the very least, it suggested that an education researcher should investigate what occurs in the course of teaching. Before we parted he mentioned that he would be glad to be of assistance, whenever I was ready to begin research on high school teachers. It surprised him when I called back a month later to ask for his help, but he kept his promise. He became an important source for information. He is the teacher I call Andy Abraham.

My concern was to find out how teachers do their work and what they think about it, particularly in the place I have called Truman High School. To do this research I relied upon the ethnographic techniques of participant observation and interview, following the methodological and theoretical standards suggested by George Spindler (1982) and Gary Wehlage (1981). The perspective I took within this method of research is what George Homans (1950) and Louis Smith (1986) have called "natural history." This means I tried to interfere as little as possible with the events unfolding naturally in the setting, while recording concrete and historical descriptions of persons and pertinent events in their lives.

In order to study the occupation of teaching, I moved into the town I call Rillton, where Mr. Abraham worked, and got a job as a teacher, renting an apartment at the edge of town. For two days out of the week I worked as an English teacher at Truman High School. During the other three days, I was in the building doing interviews and observations with the teachers who had volunteered to participate in the research. Most people were eager to tell me their stories once they learned of my interest in the conduct of teachers. The school authorities gave me permission to do the research, and I kept the people who became participants informed of my intentions.

At night and on weekends, I transcribed the notes, searched for ways to combine descriptive detail into categories, and thought about the different explanations for what I was finding. Following to some extent James Spradley's model (1979), the stages I used for ethnographic analysis were record, transcribe, edit, identify key terms, pose hypotheses, test hypotheses, build categories, test categories, and search for themes. The analysis did not proceed in a linear fashion, as this list suggests, but rather expediently and in an open-ended manner. I tried to let the research process unfold as much as possible in response to opportunities afforded by particular situations.

I started observing Andy Abraham, who was a social studies teacher at Truman, and followed up on all of the available and reasonable leads for additional observations and interviews with both educators and townspeople. I studied a variety of settings to learn about the conduct of teachers in this community. I attended classroom lectures, lunch, faculty-lounge discussions, department meetings, school board meetings, TGIF sessions at a local bar, and commuting trips to and from work. I conducted interviews with central office administrators, school board members, the high school principal, department chairpersons, the principal's secretary, teachers, students, parents, and a variety of other people who lived in the community.

What is going on here? I adopted this as the basic research question (cf. Arendt, 1978; Kaplan, 1964). From that point on I was dependent upon the goodwill of the participants, some simple recording skills, and my own ingenuity. I developed the following, more specific questions during the early stages of the fieldwork. What are the recurring formal and informal behaviors among

these high school teachers? How do these behaviors manifest
themselves, particularly in voluntary and informal groups? How
do small groups of teachers interact? What are the effects on
the curriculum of the school? Before examining more closely
the workplace culture of these teachers, it will be useful to look
at the town of Rillton and consider some details of the teachers'
situation there.

Rillton, USA

Rillton is not the real name of the town, but it stands for a real
place. I have masked certain identifying details to prevent disclo-
sure, while retaining features common to communities such as
this one that make important contributions to the school environ-
ment. As in cities and towns elsewhere in the United States, the
citizens of Rillton had a deep sense of pride in their community.
They believed strongly in the work ethic, valued highly the personal ownership of land and homes, expressed support for their
community by buying goods and services from local merchants,
and actively participated in their religious and recreational organizations. The teachers who became a part of this research felt
the influence of the community of Rillton. They either identified
with the values of Rillton's citizens or rejected them.

The roads to Rillton were long, straight, two-lane state highways. There was a large metropolitan area located more than 100
miles to the east. The nearest interstate highway was more than 50
miles away. Where two state highways met at the center of town
was the town square, with its large, grassy lawn. Located in a
midwestern state, Rillton had about 25,000 residents in 1980.
While Rillton's population was getting larger (a 2.5% increase
from 1970 to 1980), it had not realized the rapid growth that was
occurring during the same decade in towns located in the other
regions of the country.

There had been immigrants among the settlers who founded
the original town of Rillton, and its citizens continued to welcome
new groups of immigrants. Most of the oldest families in Rillton
were of European extraction. Their ancestors had come to the area
in search of work or of land for farming. The first to arrive had
drifted there in the 1820s from the eastern states. Many of the
later arrivals were foreign-born—Irish, Italian, Jewish, German,

Norwegian, and Polish. A small number of African-American families settled there in the 1920s. As these later groups of people arrived, they created ethnic enclaves on the fringes of Rillton. After the close of the Vietnam War in 1973, the religious organizations of Rillton helped twelve families of Vietnamese refugees to settle in the community.

The people of Rillton spoke with pride about what the "industrial giants" did for their community. Rillton's chief industry at this time was food processing. According to the Rillton Chamber of Commerce, "logging, lumbering, and farming preceded the diversified cannery; the former led naturally to the latter due to the history of agriculture in the region." Soon after the logging ended, some entrepreneurial community leaders established the food-processing plant, an accomplishment of considerable importance, for it replaced labor-intensive, seasonal work with permanent, indoor jobs.

Men and women directly involved with the food-processing industry rotated among three shifts, worked weekends on an "on-off" basis, and kept the plant operating twenty-four hours per day. In the air was an odor that seemed repulsive to an outsider. To the people whose livelihoods were connected to the cannery—a local realtor for example—"it smells like money." From the president of the cannery came the assurance that "you get used to it after a while." To him and all who helped manage the plant, the odor was an unfortunate but nonetheless necessary aspect of their work. There were a number of other industries in the Rillton area, but none of these had the stature and stability of the food-processing plant.

The residents maintained that one could find in Rillton almost all the goods and services needed for a good life and a good living. They would also point out that the service was friendly and personal. There was a new shopping mall, a downtown area for shopping, and three large shopping plazas. Despite the popularity of malls and shopping centers, a few mom and pop grocery stores offered their personalized style of business in the ethnic neighborhoods. In these stores, business was brisk not so much for brand-name products as for custom-made sausages and hams or relishes, sauces, and pies that were made from old family recipes. There were a technical college, a hospital, two dental clinics, a medical clinic, a mental health clinic, three fully equipped fire stations, and a police department. City government consisted of a mayor and a city council. Rillton had an airport and two bus stations offering nationwide charter service and regional transportation.

Despite appearances to the contrary, Rillton had social problems that were common to other communities. Through the news media, local citizens were made aware of their own increasing divorce rate, transformation of the family because of more mothers working outside the home, standard family need for a dual income, shortage of high-quality day care, high incidence of alcoholism and drug abuse, and a crime rate for felonies that was above the national average for a town of this size. While not precipitating a crisis, these trends were nonetheless of concern to all sectors of Rillton's social strata. Its institutions offered what help they could.

Forty houses of worship in the vicinity of Rillton offered religious services for Catholics, Jews, and Protestants. That the townspeople held their religious faiths in high regard was evident in the steeples that rose above all of the other buildings in town. The churches and synagogues offered banquets, bingo games, and bazaars for charitable purposes throughout the year, and those events were well attended. There were also year-round recreational activities. The outdoor and indoor sports activities included those that are common to American communities: slow-pitch softball, baseball, tennis, swimming, fishing, deer hunting, dirt-bike racing, stock-car racing, bowling, racketball, running, camping, snowmobiling, and cross-country skiing.

That Rillton's citizens took their sporting events seriously was especially evident during the deer-hunting season. The deer-hunting party was a major social event during the fall; some local families considered it as important as national and religious holidays. During the deer-hunting season, any high school student who had obtained a valid deer-hunting license and written permission from parents could be excused from school for the entire week. Although they had to make up whatever assignments the teachers scheduled for that week, many students—both boys and girls—took advantage of the opportunity to go deer hunting in November with relatives and friends.

The teachers at Truman High School constituted a small workforce within the community of Rillton. The work schedule of teachers was different from that of people working in business or industry, but it was more or less typical of schools: a five-day work week, 180 days of work per year, holidays off, Christmas break, and summer vacation. On the whole, teachers pursued interests during their time off that conformed with those of other adults in the area. Containing none of the restrictions placed by communities on teacher activity in an earlier day (cf. Counts, 1952; Krug, 1972), the life of a teacher in Rillton was much like that of other adults in the community. Despite some important differences, their lives appeared to have much in common not only with the cannery workers but also with bankers, insurance agents, and construction workers.

While many teachers did go deer hunting on weekends during the season, they could not get released from their contracted weekday responsibilities in the schools. Unlike the workers in the cannery, the teachers had little or no chance to engage in most of the daytime recreational activities during the fall, winter, and spring. These other workers had some choice about when they could take a vacation. The teachers took their vacations in accordance with the work schedule at Truman. Between September and May there were days off for legal holidays, teachers' convention, and snow days. Any other days away from teaching were taken in accordance with the bargaining agreement or were secret escapes (see Chapter 5). Oddly enough, the teachers had more restrictions than the plant workers in terms of vacation times and flexibility of work schedule.

During the schoolday teachers' work consisted primarily of educating high school students, and the values of Rillton entered the school through the students and influenced the education program. Some teachers accepted these values, such as sporting events, demonstrating their acceptance by involvement in co-curricular activities and by living in the town. Other teachers rejected certain values of Rillton, showing their rejection by avoiding co-curricular involvement and by living in a neighboring town. Among the social studies teachers, at least, the decision to live outside the district signified one's membership in a particular faculty subgroup and resistance to particular school and community values (cf. Gracey, 1972).

The majority of the professional and classified personnel working for the public school district of Rillton lived within the town of Rillton and they had homes in the better-off areas. There was even a street unofficially renamed "Teacher's Row" because of the number of administrators and teachers who had moved into homes there near one another. Some staff members lived in the small towns outside of Rillton that were located within the school district. Others lived on farms or in homes out in the countryside within the area served by the school district.

The seventy professional and classified employees of Rillton's public school system who lived outside of the school district constituted about 25 percent of the total workforce. Of these, nearly half lived in or near Idolville, a larger town approximately 30 miles east of Rillton. These people made it a point to live outside of the school district's boundaries, despite the central office administrators' continual efforts to encourage all employees to live within the boundary lines. Having a residence in another school district meant, among other things, that these people could not cast a vote during local school board elections, public referenda, and mayoral races.

In his research of "school and community" relations in a place called Mansfield (a town that was one-tenth the size of Rillton), Alan Peshkin (1978) reported that teachers were aware of the problems of living in the district where they taught but believed the advantages outweighed the disadvantages: "harmony . . . is one signal attribute of the school-community relationship in Mansfield" (p. 99). Truman's social studies teachers, by contrast, were split over this matter. One group liked the town and would say much the same as what Mansfield's teachers would say. The other group preferred to live in Idolville, for doing so meant little or no involvement with co-curricular activities and fewer calls from students about assignments or grades. To the latter, Rillton was where the job had to be done.

Both the faculty and the administration were critical of the teachers who chose to live outside the Rillton school district. One of the teachers, Craig Zack, had this to say about the workplace mentality, which he thought was typical of commuters to Idolville:

> I look at my colleagues who wait down at the front door for the clock to mark 3:45 P.M. for the end of the day. I think we should not work with time limits like this. The kids know who's here and who's not, and this time for involvement can build the special relationship with the students that you have to have as a teacher.

The colleagues referred to in the above quote were teachers who commuted to Idolville. In the opinion of teachers like Mr. Zack, commuters were more attuned to the end of the workday stipulated by the teaching contract, because of the long drive, than faculty who were residents of Rillton. Zack and the others who made Rillton their home believed that a teacher's work did not end at 3:45 P.M. They expressed a willingness to "show concern with kids" whether they were lecturing in the classroom, coaching some sport, walking downtown, or relaxing at home. In short, teachers who lived in Rillton expressed the belief that their "number-one concern is kids." Having a home in Rillton made them available to kids at all times.

This view from teachers about their homesite was parallel to the view of the administration. A director of curriculum had this to say about teachers who lived outside the school district:

> The exposure outside of the classroom after hours is good, if for nothing else, to build relationships that you wouldn't get if you were confined to the classroom. The exposure on Friday night at athletic events acquaints you with the community. The payoff for teachers: recognition and acceptance. It is a fact that in many schools the source of community interest revolves around athletics. All you have to do is go to an Idolville and Rillton standoff and see the kids and parents involved in a win-or-lose situation. This puts the teacher, especially the coach, in the limelight. If you live in Idolville, how many times are you going to drive over here for these games? We have something going on all of the time at the high school.

Principals and central office personnel believed that the advantages of living within the district outweighed the disadvantages. As the above quote indicates, administrators believed it was important for teachers to be visible to people in Rillton. If teachers made Rillton their home, they would shop in its stores, join local clubs, and vote during local elections. Also, when a principal asked for volunteers to help direct co-curricular activities, the distance a faculty member would have to commute would not be a stated or implied excuse for not volunteering. The administrators' belief stemmed from the perceived expectations of Rillton's citizens about their public school officials. Administrators saw themselves as victims of community expectations over which they felt they had little control, while teachers typically viewed administrators as taking sides with the school board and influential citizens of Rillton.

Rillton parents did not express disapproval of teachers' choosing to live outside of the school district. However, these parents

did expect teachers to support both the academic and co-curricular program of the school, and they maintained a general interest
in the conduct of teachers. As one parent pointed out, the details of
teachers' lives eventually became known to anyone with an interest in teacher activity: "You are surprised at how much a parent
can find out about a teacher. Just to give you an example, I think it
was Art Heidman who it was said practically flunked out of
college." Parents said that they had called the principal in response to rumor or evidence that teachers were presenting subject
matter they found inappropriate, offensive, or damaging for high
school students. Parents also knew which of the teachers attended
games or performances and which teachers served as coaches or
sponsors. The teachers who commuted to work from Idolville
would sponsor student clubs and occasionally attend athletic
events, but they would not serve as chaperones or coaches. If
parents became irate over what they thought was misconduct of
local teachers (no matter how far away the supposed misconduct
occurred), they were quick to phone or write of it to the administration or school board. The building principal and central office
administrators acknowledged that they received these complaints.

At issue here is the formal role expectation of teachers. The
parents wanted the school to offer academic and co-curricular
programs and made this dual interest known to the administration and the school board. These authorities for the school encouraged teachers to assume responsibility in both areas of interest.
The involvement in co-curricular work constituted an important
difference between teachers. In the social studies department of
the high school, the teachers responded by either accepting or
rejecting the dual-role expectation. Those teachers who thought of
their formal role as, above all else, subject-matter specialization
turned down most requests that they participate in co-curricular
activities, using residence in Idolville as an excuse. Others perceived their formal role to include co-curricular participation as
well as teaching and made Rillton their home in order to facilitate
involvement in the former. These teachers could thus receive recognition on each account, but especially for their co-curricular
involvement.

Taking into consideration that some of the sports activities
offered by the local school district supported the recreational program available in the community, the coaches on the staff either
introduced some of the children living in the area to many of these
sports activities or they developed the skills of the youngsters

further as they were going through the grades. The townspeople witnessed the effects of the coaches' work with students during games and read in the local newspaper about victories, defeats, strategies, awards banquets, and so on. Administrators appreciated this public relations work by coaches, because the townspeople told the administrators that they wanted to see their boys and girls go to state tournaments. Cusick (1983) traced the suburban high school principal's power to the benefits he or she could give to teachers who helped out with extracurricular activities. And in towns like Rillton, the school's role as a source of community solidarity is as or more important than its role in promoting academic studies.

Teachers who turned down opportunities to work in the co-curricular programs could be rewarded only for their good work in fostering student achievement in the school's academic program. That kind of reward, however, is less available than are the rewards of a winning team or a trophy standing in a place of honor in the principal's office. Research shows that teachers consider psychic rewards to be important for job satisfaction, but such rewards are harder to come by (Boyer, 1983; Lortie, 1975; Maeroff, 1988; Sizer, 1985). My research indicates that some teachers will search for psychic rewards in co-curricular activities. Andy Abraham summed it up cynically with, "All the rewards go to the PR (public relations) people." He and a number of other teachers believed that subject-matter specialists realized too little reward and recognition for their work.

This perceived lack of recognition and reward for subject-matter specialists led to feelings of cynicism and hostility toward the institution among teachers like Mr. Abraham. Teachers adopted this view because while school authorities expected teachers to embrace the dual-role expectation, they provided little or no assistance in mediating the apparent conflicts associated with a teacher's service in both the academic and co-curricular programs. Even teachers who were active in the co-curricular program were discontented, because their involvement as coaches and sponsors tended to interfere with their role expectations for teaching.

Teachers expressed their antagonism about the perceived conflict in role expectations toward both formal and informal organizations of the school. The formal organization of the school consisted of the school board, central office administrators, building principal, guidance personnel, and the academic departments.

The informal organization of the social studies department was comprised of two primary, opposing groups—Academics and Coaches. Within these informal subgroups teachers helped one another make decisions about matters of importance, such as where to live, which educational programs to endorse, and what activities to pursue, avoid, or resist. I shall deal first with the school's formal organization and its influence on the teachers' lives at the time of this research.

Truman High School

In many respects the Rillton public school system was typical. At the top of the formal organization was a superintendent. Beneath him were two assistant superintendents, several specialized curriculum directors, and building-level principals. The Rillton Board of Education reviewed all proposals, grievances, collective bargaining sessions, and so forth. Based to some extent upon their own judgment and to a greater or lesser extent upon the professional advice of the superintendent, they either accepted or rejected what was put before them. The administration and the school board saw to it that the teachers offered a public school education in Rillton that balanced the needs and interests of professional educators with those of the community.

The Rillton Public School District had one high school for grades 10–12, two junior high schools for grades 7–9, and twelve elementary schools for grades K–6. The estimated operating budget for the 1980–81 school year in Rillton was nearly $15 million, a fact that was becoming more and more troublesome for both the educators and the community. A comparison of total annual operating budgets for the Rillton Public School District for the past three years showed an 11 percent increase per year. New building construction, remodeling, expansion of services, and specialized personnel accounted for the progressive increase in school expenses. Local taxpayers were not accustomed to raising their school tax levy on a regular basis. The more vocal members of the community made their opposition to continued escalation of the school tax known to the school board and administrators. Through local referenda, letters, and speeches at school board meetings, influential members of the community had given the school authorities notice that the school budget was to be cut back to prevent increases in local taxes.

According to newspaper editorials, the community appreciated Truman High School but saw it as contributing to the problem of "rapidly escalating costs for education" for at least two reasons: recent building construction and declining enrollment. Truman High School was a modern structure that the community had planned and built during the previous five years. It was a two-story, red brick building with such facilities as regular classrooms, science labs, an instructional materials center (IMC), cafeteria, vocational and technical shops, and so on. The professional staff of the high school included the principal and two assistant principals, 100 full-time teachers, five counselors, ten secretaries, and fifteen study hall aides.

Student enrollment in the Rillton Public School District was continuing to decline. The fall 1980 enrollment at Truman (1,923) was nearly the same as it had been during the 1973–74 school year (1,941). The peak enrollment at the high school (1,981) had occurred in the 1978–79 school year. Since the administration expected the enrollment decline—most notable then at the high school level—to continue, their response was to "shift" or lay off teachers so as to keep operating costs at a level acceptable to the school board and the community. This strategy effectively subdued, for the time being, the outcry from the community, but it raised rancor among teachers.

The word *shift* was a reference to the principal's assignment of disliked or incompetent teachers to less desirable classes at the high school or transfer to the junior high school, where student enrollment had stabilized at a higher level. A high school teacher's morale did not receive a boost from being shifted into the junior high school. Teachers would razz someone they disliked who was targeted for a transfer to a lower level and would try to protect favored colleagues from being shifted. These informal behaviors helped certain teachers cope with their actual or potential assignment to a lower level.

In most school districts teachers with the least seniority receive the non-renewal notices first. However, because the community placed a high value on athletic competition in football, basketball, and baseball, the administration felt obliged to add a clause in the bargaining contract that exempted from layoff teachers who also coached. This show of preference for coaching outraged the teachers who considered themselves first and foremost subject-matter specialists. They turned to their formal and informal organizations for help. The obvious formal organization to turn to was the local teachers' union. With help from their union representative, subject-matter specialists hoped to negotiate a contract that favored a layoff policy having seniority as the sole criterion. They failed in this endeavor.

Bargaining between the Rillton Education Association and the Rillton Board of Education went into closed session on this and related issues. At the last meeting the superintendent gave an ominous statement to the teachers: "For the record, we intend to exempt teachers from layoff in such a way that we can maintain both the academic program and the co-curricular program." The position of the administration (with assent from the school board) was this: Truly worthy educational endeavors are only those that embrace both classroom instruction and co-curricular programs. Most notable among the latter were competitive sports, such as baseball, basketball, football, and wrestling. To the chagrin of some teachers, the district would not award additional compensation for extra scholarly study in a subject-matter specialty. Also, in cases where a layoff was imminent, a teacher's history of involvement with co-curricular activities could make the difference between losing and keeping the job.

On the informal level subject-matter specialists responded by repudiating those who coached as well as taught and regarding skeptically the formal authority structure for the school. Since even the union could not offer guarantees for preferred work assignments and job security, these teachers tended to rely upon one another for protection from an institutional system that they saw as bypassing their needs and establishing policy that threatened their continuance at the school.

Contrary to what one would think, the teachers who coached were not in such good standing with the administration that their informal organization was any less important to their work. One could argue that there was a difference in form, but not in substance. Membership in the informal group was just as important to these teachers as it was to those who valued subject-matter specialty more highly. Neither subgroup of the social studies faculty at Truman enjoyed privileged status.

More to the point, the problem of declining enrollments served to exacerbate the older and, for the teachers at least, more serious problems of conflict in role expectations for teaching at Truman. Although the noncoaching teachers considered themselves better prepared as "subject-matter specialists," all of the teachers were well prepared in academic subjects and wanted very much to teach. The adults in Rillton wanted teachers to offer instruction in academic subjects, but they also put a high value on co-curricular activities. The teachers believed that it was exceedingly difficult to sustain a high quality of work in both spheres of activity without a substantive revision in the definition of work, including the daily schedule.

The quality of life experienced in school by the teacher on a day-by-day basis and the question of whether or not the teacher would be renewed, transferred, or shifted at any time depended to a great extent upon the people occupying positions of authority. But the persons holding these positions of authority, such as the principal and the two assistant principals, were relatively ineffective in addressing and resolving problems central to teaching in the secondary school. Thus the social studies teachers counted on their voluntary, informal organizations to provide a kind of buffer in dealing with their personal and professional problems.

The principal was responsible for administering the high school program for Rillton at the building level. Relationships between the principals and the teachers (other than chance meetings) were generally of two kinds: semiannual evaluations and private conferences. Teachers in the social studies department found that this state of affairs reflected a lack of commitment to responsible leadership.

School policy required that the principal evaluate teachers on a semiannual basis. Teachers usually received advance notice that a principal would be observing and evaluating classroom work for one forty-seven-minute period on a particular day late in the semester. Afterwards, the principal would send a report to the teacher and file two other copies—one in the principal's office and the other in the central office.

Contrary to their desires, though, teachers had little expectation that they would find anything rewarding to their egos in the report. When I asked Andy Abraham about the evaluations, he gave this explanation of the process and its outcome:

> An assistant principal will spend an hour in our classrooms once or twice a year. The critical remarks that we get show what they look for: dressed too informally, forgot to post the absentee report, voice too loud, wait longer for answers, failed to call on a student. It's all petty stuff. One time the

lecture might be great and the next time poor, but the marks show no difference. Administrators are not in the classrooms enough to know what's really going on.

Classroom observations showed that this criticism seemed to have merit, for what passed as acceptable instructional methods and materials varied from one teacher's assigning students to read and answer questions at the end of every chapter while he worked out crossword puzzles, to another teacher's delivering a rousing lecture on the issue of gun control. Cusick (1983) writes that "matters of attendance, discipline, and public relations take up the greatest part of the supervisory and administrative resources in public secondary schools" (p. 5). It may be that since control of students (not quality of teaching) was the key factor at Truman, administrators would consider both of the above instances to be equally acceptable as instructional methods.

The building principal readily admitted that he had far fewer opportunities to evaluate and provide professional guidance to his teachers than he desired, due to an excess of responsibilities handed down from the central office. When teachers sought ideas for classroom instruction or reinforcement of methods that seemed to be producing the desired outcome of instruction, they looked to certain of their colleagues. On a number of occasions I observed teachers discussing with one another the quality of their lectures or other methods they were using or thinking of using. When I asked about the role of the building principal and his assistants in relation to the formal routines of teaching, teachers remarked that they did not have discussions about content or methods with their principals.

It was through private conferences rather than through formal evaluations that the administrators got to know the teachers. A teacher would come to the building principal or one of the assistants for a variety of reasons, but it was usually for defense or shelter. A teacher might believe that the counselors or special education personnel had assigned too many unruly students to a class, and therefore wanted some of them removed. For example, Clifford Harris would first complain about the "low-level" students to the special education teachers when he met them in the hallways; then, if the specialists did nothing to relieve him, he complained to the assistant principal in charge of student discipline. After one of these meetings with the assistant principal, he reported his complaint to me as follows: "I have so goddamn many low-level kids—and I'm sorry for coming down on the specialists—but I don't feel competent to deal with their emotional problems and screwy behavior in the classroom."

If a student's parents took offense at what was presented in class to their youngster, the teachers expected that the administration would stand behind them. This defense by the administration was not guaranteed. For example, when an irate parent complained to the building principal that Art Heidman's lecture on gun control upset her daughter, the principal informed Mr. Heidman that he apologized for him and then chided him for being "insensitive."

When some personal disaster occurred, the teacher sought and obtained relief from professional responsibilities—usually immediately. Yet while teachers expected the administrators to be their allies whenever they needed defense or shelter from school-related matters, there was no assurance that the administrators would respond in this manner. To illustrate, when Clayton Samuels slapped a student for saying "fuck you" to him in class, he was informed by the assistant principal in charge of student discipline that the use of corporal punishment was against school policy and warned not to resort to it in the future. Venting his frustration, Samuels told two of his colleagues:

> That's a bunch of bullshit. The damn rules are set up in favor of the kids. They know it and get away with it all the time. I'm not going to stand for it. I got a whole room full of those characters and if I let one of them say "fuck you" to me, they'll all do it. I can't get *anything* from that office, because all those people are so afraid of a lawsuit. I'm not arguing for physical abuse; I'm saying that a slap on the face isn't out of line when some student calls you a name or says what this student said in the classroom.

Questions about formal routines of teaching, including the handling of discipline problems, were topics that teachers took up with colleagues, not with the building principal or his assistants. In the example above, the teacher's use of physical force was not approved of by the school authorities. Later, he found teachers interested in his problem and, eventually, suggestions for resolving the problem and coping with the administration.

Teachers who approached the principal for endorsement of new programs could expect a rebuff. For example, when Calvin Miller wanted to initiate a program promoting more involvement between the elementary students and their parents during after-school hours, he was "shot out of the saddle" because he would have needed twelve days off from school. Mr. Miller explained the incident further:

> I had to get the elementary school principal's approval, so I first asked my principal. He said he heard a lot of complaints that high school teachers always go down and tell the elementary people what to do. Then, he said that the elementary principals are very busy in the spring. At the end of meeting he told me he'd get back to me, but he hasn't. It has been two weeks now. I think his explanation is an attempt to make me drop it.

This remark is representative of the critical stance taken by many teachers toward the administration. Mary Metz (1984) reports a similar response among male teachers toward the administration in a middle school: "They proclaimed that when they had inventive ideas these were vetoed by the Administrator in Charge or bogged down in logistical difficulties or administrative inaction" (p. 8). When discussing implementation of curriculum plans, Truman's teachers, like those Metz observed, usually spoke about the administration in tones of anger and frustration.

For example, the social studies teachers expressed the desire to have an assistant principal attend their department meetings so a school authority could resolve conflicts between the two factions over curriculum plans. In effect, had it happened, this move would have short-circuited the political process common to the two informal groups. But the assistant principal did not attend and did not explain himself. His absence frustrated some of the teachers. They believed that the assistant principal, like the other administrators, was ineffectual with respect to providing leadership that had a direct impact on their teaching. The strength of their conviction about the administration tended to inhibit the social studies teachers from initiating substantive action on the curriculum plan.

It was not that the principal ignored teachers' requests for defense and shelter. Rather, the size of the high school and the numerous administrative responsibilities limited his chances of meeting requests from the faculty. There were instances when his action rescued teachers from embarrassment or ruin as, for example, when Alfred Moore came to him disturbed about the death of a close relative. At the risk of "catching some flack" from the central office administrators, the principal made immediate arrangements for Mr. Moore to spend ten days recovering. In the words of Mr. Moore, the principal's action was "nothing short of heroic." However, this was not part of a pattern of activity common to administrators; it merely indicated inconsistent treatment of teachers' problems.

The following explanation from Andy Abraham about the relationship between himself and his principal captured its essence.

> The principal is an important variable in the school, but he's limited. He can make it uncomfortable by being petty, but if you insulate yourself from that, he doesn't have much greater effect on you than that, because he's too busy. He can't keep on top of you in a meaningful way.

The principal was not in a position to question the teachers' expertise in subject matter, and, because subject-matter knowledge had so much to do with explaining the teacher's work within the school, the principal could only watch for situations rife with opportunities for teachers to break the rules. Then the principal could be "petty." So long as teachers maintained a satisfactory level of competence with special subject matter and were not caught breaking the rules, they felt insulated from the principal.

The teachers believed that the principal's removal from their daily interactions with students and colleagues prevented him from understanding the problems they confronted. As a result, they defined the scheduled meetings between themselves and the principal as "meaningless ritual." Although informal meetings between a teacher and the principal sometimes produced results favorable to the teacher, by and large it was the informal teacher groups to which teachers went for discussion and resolution of their problems. This state of affairs contributed to the teachers' dependency upon their small group. The general lack of supervision from the principal and the relative independence of the teachers led to the development and use of some unprofessional teaching behaviors.

Another institutional structure that was supposed to have a positive influence on the work of teachers was the Guidance Office, out of which the counselors and specialists worked. A primary responsibility of the guidance personnel was to place students in courses that matched their needs and interests. They used course descriptions and prerequisites from teachers, cumulative record files, recommendations from junior high school teachers, and their own judgment about the students and the teachers to help students satisfy requirements for the high school diploma. On an official level, teachers had little or no say in regard to the enrollment of students in classes, a policy that vexed teachers in the social studies department.

The Guidance Office had evolved four classifications for students: low level, low ability, average ability, and above-average ability. Teachers used the term *low levels* in reference to students that the counselors transferred into the regular classrooms from special education classrooms. In education jargon, they were "mainstreamed." Low-level students were generally unpopular among teachers because the teachers believed their behavior and attitude were intolerably deviant and their academic performance was well below average. One teacher expressed a representative opinion of these students as follows:

> I had a couple of low levels four or five years ago. I got rid of them. They thoroughly, 100 percent, frustrated me. They wouldn't let me teach. They are so far from teachable human beings it's unbelievable. Here's one example: some guy brought an old muffler to class and started passing it around to the kids while I was talking. There was no way I could hold their attention. Now, if I had to have them in a class, I wouldn't even try to teach the regular course content. I'd teach reading, writing, and math. They'd get a test every day and the first one to lip off I'd throw out on the spot.

When asked in interviews about their work with low-level students, teachers expressed discontent over what they perceived to be inappropriate practice by counselors and special education teachers. Courses were available to match the different ability groups, but the counselors' placement of low-level students put emphasis on selection of a teacher. The presence of such students in a classroom stigmatized a teacher as one who was less competent than others in knowledge of subject matter and methods of teaching.

Counselors were either liked or disliked by teachers, depending upon which class—sophomore, junior, or senior—they were enrolling in teachers' courses. The sophomore students not only had their full complement of identified and unidentified low-level students; as a group they had not become acclimated to the high school community and were not wanted by most teachers. In the opinion of the teachers, sophomores were "easily distracted and [exhibited] bad behavior problems." In fact, social studies teachers described whole classes of sophomores as "squirrelly." According to Andy Abraham, the principal's assignment of sophomore-level classes to a teacher, as with the low levels by the counselors, was "the shit detail for teachers." These teachers believed that a counselor's involvement through enrollment activities showed complicity with the principal's decision.

The social studies teachers had developed three types of responses to the policies and practices of counselors and specialists. One was to concentrate efforts on securing and defending required senior-level and college-prep courses. Another response was to develop a rationale for accepting low-level students, a move that kept the accepting teachers on equal footing with teachers who rejected the students. The third response concerned the actual presence of low-level students in the classroom—some teachers had evolved effective techniques for preventing misbehavior among all their students, but especially the low-level ones.

One might expect that at the lowest level of the school's formal organization, the teachers would perceive their needs to be met in a satisfactory manner. This was not the case in the social studies department at Truman. The department chairperson was the superordinate whose decisions were to affect the teacher's life in a most direct manner. This position was the last institutional structure that could have had some influence on the teacher's work in the classroom. However, the teachers noted that there was an ironic twist: Just as inactivity on the part of the chairperson could be frustrating and support a bad workplace mentality, so too, could the chairperson's activity, when directed in particular channels.

The previous chairperson of the social studies department, Alex Bates, was a strong-willed person who exercised authority and tended to favor one informal group within the department over the other. Mr. Bates argued against the principal's preference for hiring social studies teachers who were willing to serve as coaches. He also pushed, against the interests of these teachers, for adoption of curriculum materials he favored for social studies instruction. The department adopted the new materials, but the spurned teachers used these materials grudgingly.

Alex Bates had pursued curriculum development with firm convictions about what constituted appropriate social studies subject matter. In contrast, the next department chairperson, Calvin Miller, said that he had had the chairmanship position "dumped into his lap" after Alex Bates resigned from teaching at Truman; he preferred not to take a directive role, but instead allowed the different factions within the department to vie for control over decisions that would affect all of them. This state of affairs contributed to the frustration of the teachers and the continual development of two opposing informal groups within the department.

The Social Studies Department

The social studies department constituted the principal involuntary element in the teachers' formal organization. In fact, the only times when all of the social studies teachers could be found together were the weekly department meetings scheduled by the department chairperson and required by the administration.

As the number of students enrolled at Truman increased, so did the number of social studies department members. Central office hiring records indicated that during the twenty years from 1960 to 1980 the department had added eight new teachers, bringing the total to fourteen. Figure 2.1 lists department members alphabetically (by pseudonyms), arranged by clique. Most of these teachers had worked ten or more years at Truman. Most new faculty hired during Alex Bates's tenure as chairperson became members of the Academic clique, accounting for the slight imbalance. But although the Academic clique outnumbered the Coach clique, the Coaches corrected this difference through networking in other departments.

As a formal organization, the social studies department was ineffective in addressing and resolving professional issues of importance to individuals and groups of teachers. For instance, when Carl Stevens, who was under consideration for layoff, argued during a meeting that they should discuss the issue openly so that everyone would know the different positions, the others listened in

FIGURE 2.1. *The Social Studies Department*

Academic Clique	Coach Clique
Andy Abraham	Cora Chapin
Amy Bentley	Clifford Harris
Alex Bates (former chairman)	Curtis Jasper (recently retired)
Anthony Finley	Calvin Miller (current chairman)
Arthur Heidman	Clayton Samuels
Alfred Moore	Carl Stevens
Alvin Schumacher	Craig Zack
Alan Silvius	
Arnold Wilkes	

stony silence. Issues like layoffs were handled by the informal groups, and Mr. Stevens, only recently hired, did not have a secure relationship with other members of the Coach clique. With his voice breaking, he ended his speech with, "That's all I wanted to say; thank you." No one else said anything about the matter.

Usually, the main topic of discussion at department meetings was further development of the social studies curriculum. A consensus held that these meetings accomplished nothing of substance. Frustration with this formal organization's failure to accomplish anything meaningful led Alan Silvius to exclaim, "What I am going to do is go in my room, close my door, and do whatever the fuck I want." Such individualism, as Lortie (1975) pointed out, may be important, for teachers need to learn "personal ways to cope with provocation and anger, guilt and shame." The point is that there are aspects of the job for which the formal organization provides no relief mechanisms. The faculty subculture in the social studies department at Truman played a part in developing strategies that helped individuals cope with onerous aspects of teaching.

Despite exclamations like that reported above, teachers were dependent on one another. Down the hall from every teacher's door was another teacher in another classroom with similar problems. Interaction with these others was a crucial form of support for social studies teachers at Truman. A teacher who really acted independently (and one tried) would not only lack the support ostensibly offered by the formal organization of the school, but would be cutoff from the only existing and meaningful support system for teachers—the informal group—and would find working in the school an exceedingly lonely, oppressive, and frustrating experience.

Although the purpose of the school's formal organization was to facilitate the education program at Truman, teachers found it difficult to think of themselves as partners with the administration. (The department chairperson, a teacher/administrator, was the only exception.) As is common in other high schools, the administration was responsible for maintaining a system that upheld the interests of both the educators and the local community. The superintendent expressed his position as follows:

> It is important to maintain both the academic program and the co-curricular program. Just where the emphasis will lie on a given concern is a judgment of what is in the best interest of the school district: what is more valuable for the overall good of the school. I reserve the right to argue that issue.

In other words, decision making in this school system followed a top-down, low-interaction pattern common among secondary schools and prevalent in business and industry. Teachers felt the effects of the system most directly and frequently at the level of the academic department. Their response to the lack of collaboration was to depend upon their small groups for forming an idea about the role and activity of the teacher. To sustain themselves in their dual work role, Truman's social studies teachers had evolved formal and informal routines to press students for high achievement in the classroom and on the field.

This dual role for teachers split Truman's social studies department into the Academics and Coaches. The authorities for the school chose not to resolve this issue or to relieve teachers of their frustrations about the discontinuities in perceived role expectations. Although Cusick (1983) reports that "one cannot dichotomize the staff of that or any other high school into 'academically minded' and 'activity minded' teachers" (p. 94), teachers in the social studies department of Truman divided themselves along such lines and believed that the administration wanted teachers to be both. The work schedule in the school intensified the problem. Those in positions of authority had little contact with students. Teachers were involved directly and continuously with educating students, but they had little authority. The hierarchical work structure militated against collaborative planning among teachers and administrators and promoted formal and informal teacher behaviors that were independent and self-serving.

Summary

I have tried to convey in this chapter a general impression of Rillton, the community where the teachers worked, and of Truman High School. The selection of details should indicate that Rillton was a relatively stable community. The people who called it home shopped in its stores, supported their local organizations, and welcomed newcomers. The teachers who worked at Truman High School were no less welcome in the community than other groups of workers. The townspeople, like taxpayers and parents elsewhere in the nation, believed that the work of public school teachers should include involvement not only in the academic program, but also in the co-curricular activities.

This idea of a dual role for the teacher was acceptable to some teachers in the social studies department but unacceptable to others. However, all of the teachers believed that unless there were changes in the definition of work it would be very difficult, if not impossible, to excel in both areas. Moreover, the district's problems with an escalating budget and declining enrollment put pressure on central office administrators to cut costs. The policy adopted by the administration, which included provisions for non-renewal and shifting, contrasted sharply with Rillton's values— chiefly, stability and local support. This dichotomy disturbed the teachers, encouraging them to look more and more toward their informal groups for support and relief.

It would be of little interest if this situation simply begged for a solution to the conflict over whose idea about work should dominate. A serious difference of opinion rarely finds resolution easily. Teachers, like other workers, will develop ideas about their work roles in response to the circumstances they face on a daily basis at work (see McLaughlin & Yee, 1988). This condition involves teachers in a process of reflective thinking at the levels of the individual and of the group. The results include developing a role expectation and related activities for teaching that will work, but might not be suitable for the aims of education. Our wishes to the contrary, we should expect to find unsuitable deviation from norms of professional conduct when the teachers' perceptions of supervisors include inconsistent and unfair treatment. An appreciation of this point requires a closer look at the social studies department. In order to prepare for the later part of the discussion, I will now describe in more detail the characteristics of the two groups of teachers.

CHAPTER 3

The Cliques

On the day before classes were to begin, Rillton's school administrators held an in-service session. The meeting began at 9:00 A.M. in the high school auditorium with an official welcome back from the superintendent and a lecture on discipline from a guest speaker. Afterwards, the teachers attended faculty and department meetings. At noon the high school teachers picked up their keys and prepared their rooms for another year of teaching. It was my first day on the job, so I made plans that morning to meet Andy Abraham after work.

"Where should we meet?" I asked Mr. Abraham as we were filing into the theater for the superintendent's opening address. "Where else? I'll be waiting for you in my room," he replied. At 3:30 P.M. I rounded a corner of the second-floor hallway—lost—and saw up ahead the silhouette of a man leaning against a doorjamb. "Where the hell have you been?" he shouted. It was Andy Abraham. "It's almost time to leave," he continued. We had only fifteen minutes remaining, he explained, because he and four other teachers belonged to a car pool that departed for Idolville at 3:45 P.M. every workday.

I pulled out a list of the teachers in the social studies department and asked him to tell me something about his colleagues. Before he got started, another teacher, Art Heidman, came to the doorway, carrying his briefcase. "Let's go," he said. Mr. Abraham introduced us and told him about my question. Art Heidman had a ready-made answer. He said, "There are two kinds of teachers in this department, those who know something and those who are dumb as a post. Here comes Silvius. Let's get his opinion."

Art Heidman introduced me to Alan Silvius, who was walking toward our small group at the doorway. "What do you think of Craig Zack?" Mr. Heidman asked Mr. Silvius. "I can't stand being around him. His presence, just his presence," the latter replied. "It's like this," Art Heidman explained while turning to me, "you are going to get two views about teaching here. One from the Coaches, like Zack, and another from us. You will be struck by the contrast that you get from the other side." With that said, Mr. Heidman started walking away and told the others, "Let's go, Moore and Finley are waiting at the car." It was time for them to leave for Idolville.

During this brief introduction, Art Heidman and Alan Silvius made it clear to me that the social studies department at Truman consisted of two opposing, small groups. A teacher fulfilled an informal role expectation by adopting one group's definition of the teacher's role and by participating in the informal activities of that particular small group. Involvement in this subculture was important to a teacher, for, as Alan Silvius explained: "This group is the *only* thing that has enabled me to survive as a teacher in this high school; without that I would have been gone long ago." Teachers in both groups acted in ways that were independent of and sometimes even contrary to the expectations of school authorities.

Academics and Coaches

Since teachers, administrators, students, and parents referred to the two groups of teachers as "cliques," I also use that term. I call one clique "Academics" and the other clique "Coaches." One could tell the clique membership of a teacher by noting contrasts of paraphernalia. A Coach would carry a textbook and teacher's guide, basketball, whistle, clipboard, or duffel bag while moving from one area in school to another. An Academic would carry a book on political or economic theory, a clipping from an underground newspaper, or a documentary film on a controversial issue. These accoutrements were important keys to understanding the ethos of each clique.

For instance, Coaches gained prestige when they proved that they could "take the boys and girls to state." The display of sports paraphernalia in the classroom or hallways was a kind of visual clue a teacher could use to identify himself with this endeavor and its rewards. Partly in response, students addressed them as "Coach," regardless of their attire. However, these teachers were aware that the administration hired them to teach and gave them a separate contract to coach. They believed that "going to state" involved more than success in athletic competition. Their teaching methods—for example, following a textbook—demonstrated their reflective consideration of dual work roles and community values.

By contrast, the prestige-carrying image for the Academics was that of scholar with a penchant for criticism of culture and society. Their display of books, magazines, and films addressing controversial topics signaled their allegiance to a certain intellectual standard. They hired themselves out to teach social studies and, despite administrator preferences for teachers to become involved with co-curricular activities, had no intention of diverting their thoughts to programs they held in low esteem, such as athletics. The primary concern of the Academics was to provide instruction in college-prep courses, and their formal and informal behavior supported this idea of work. Although many students disliked these teachers because they represented a set of values foreign to the largely blue-collar culture of Rillton, these same students nonetheless accepted them. The disparate attitude may be attributed to the students' general expectation of strangeness in teachers (cf. Waller, 1932).

Where there is a primary group, there is some type of social structure (see Cooley, 1909/1921; Goffman, 1959; Whyte, 1943). Figure 3.1 presents the social structure that had evolved among those in the Academic clique after Alex Bates resigned. Andy Abraham's position was leader. His colleagues thought of him as a resourceful man, independent in judgment and, in the opinion of his followers, right most of the time. Teachers held different statuses within the Academic clique. Andy Abraham viewed Bentley, Moore, Schumacher, and Wilkes as teachers who were aspiring to full acceptance in the informal group. He thought of Heidman, Finley, and Silvius as sustained members.

FIGURE 3.1. *The Academic Clique*

Leader	Aspirers	Members
Andy Abraham	Amy Bentley	Arthur Heidman
	Alfred Moore	Anthony Finley
	Alvin Schumacher	Alan Silvius
	Arnold Wilkes	

A teacher earned status as a sustained member in the Academic clique through acceptance of Mr. Abraham's authority and consistent participation in activities that contributed to the clique's purpose. Regarding the former, an assistant superintendent remarked: "Abraham might be feared by the others in the clique." It would not have been easy to examine the teachers' fears. However, the words and actions of aspiring and sustained clique members indicated that they thought their leader was right about subject matter, methods, and administrators.

Figure 3.2 illustrates the social structure that had evolved among those in the Coach clique. Once again, the person occupying the central position, in this case Craig Zack, is shown at the top of the authority structure. There were six social studies teachers in the Coach clique, and these teachers also had two status categories. Two were seeking status as sustained members, while three others besides Craig Zack held this status at the time of the fieldwork. The leader, Mr. Zack, was the person to whom Chapin, Harris, Miller, Samuels, and Stevens went to for advice and encouragement.

Craig Zack knew more about what was going on in the Coach clique than anybody else. When a teacher assigned to the low-level classes had a problem with his students, he sought help from Craig Zack. At the lunch table in the teachers' lounge, Mr. Zack was the center of attention. When he was absent from a department meeting, arguments presented by others in the clique were ineffective against arguments from sustained members of the Academic clique. According to teachers in the Academic clique, Craig Zack was the man who "led the attack" for Coaches. Alan Silvius had this to say about Craig Zack: "Sometimes he is very calm, and sometimes something will touch him off and he is ready to rip your head off." Although one of the others in the clique might "scream and holler and pound on a desk" while presenting the case for Coaches, Silvius explained, the display was of little influence by comparison with a similar "attack" from Zack.

What accounted for the fact that Andy Abraham and Craig Zack occupied leadership positions in their respective cliques? To a great extent it was distance for Andy Abraham and rigor for Craig Zack. During the more than twenty hours spent in department meetings over the course of the school year, Andy Abraham spoke only once. Members of his clique believed others feared him because he was, in Art Heidman's words, "a very intelligent man,

FIGURE 3.2. *The Coach Clique*

Leader	Aspirers	Members
Craig Zack	Cora Chapin	Clifford Harris
	Carl Stevens	Calvin Miller
		Clayton Samuels

dynamic, a commanding presence." The aloofness Andy Abraham projected during meetings was a mannerism that all the Academics used to advantage with students, administrators, and faculty. It was part of the Academics' repertoire of supportive behavior. As the leader, Andy Abraham set the example for the others. From Craig Zack came the explanation that "he will only open up in private."

According to his peers and supervisors, Craig Zack was an outspoken man and was "running roughshod" over the teachers of low-level sophomores. When present in department meetings, he usually led the argument for curriculum development from the standpoint of the Coaches. He believed strongly that teachers had an obligation to be involved in co-curricular activities, for in his opinion it was through these that students came to know and respect their teachers. This belief and the behavior that supported it were important elements in the workplace culture specific to Coaches. To some extent the activities of Abraham and Zack became models for those who were sustained members as well as those who were aspiring to membership in either clique. Anthony Finley, for example, looked to Andy Abraham for advice. Mr. Finley had been a regular full-time social studies teacher at the high school for the past ten years.

Academics tended to keep a distance between themselves and others, especially Coaches. Andy Abraham's social relations seldom extended beyond the clique of which he was the head. Even within the Academic clique, he and the other sustained members—Finley, Silvius, and Heidman—favored meeting with one another over meeting with those who were seeking membership. Mr. Abraham, like others in his clique, seldom interacted with teachers other than while engaged in school-related activities. His out-of-school relations with teachers were largely coincidental. From time to time Abraham, Finley, Heidman, and Silvius would do something together on a weekend or a weekday evening. For instance, they might attend a lecture at the state university, take in a show at the theater, or go on a fishing trip.

Generally speaking, collegial interaction by those in the Academic clique was exclusive of other teachers in the high school. The maintenance of this behavior followed from the Academics' criticism of other teachers and rejection of Rillton's values. The Academics thought of themselves as a minority among teachers at Truman. They described other teachers as "dumb as a post," "hopeless," or "dead." They stayed aloof from the school's athletic program, put down the major industry in the area, and exchanged instructional media they classified as "radical." Participation in the activities of the Academic clique and adoption of its beliefs made trust in a small number of colleagues a crucial aspect of the Academic ethos. One's contract could be cut short if the wrong information got into the wrong hands. There was no tenure for teachers in the Rillton Public School District.

Like all other teachers in his clique, Andy Abraham sometimes had to engage in social relationships he did not enjoy, namely, with teachers in the other clique. He avoided these interactions whenever possible. Sometimes he would miss a department meeting; sometimes, instead of going to the teachers' lounge for lunch, he would eat in his room; sometimes he would go to the professional lounge in the library to relax alone. There was an interesting perception held by the Academics concerning their preference not to associate with Coaches: they believed that the mere association of an Academic with a sustained member of the Coach clique suggested that the Academic might be having second thoughts about endorsement of community values, especially placement of competitive sports above academic studies.

Students were aware of the two groups and understood in a general way the nature of the teachers' conflicts and disagreements. One graduate of Truman explained it this way: "We all knew that there was something going on between them. They would avoid each other in the halls. You would see certain teachers talk to only certain teachers, but not to others. Sometimes they would put each other down in our classes." Parents were also aware of the two cliques in the department.

Mr. Zack's base of social relations at Truman was broad by comparison with Mr. Abraham's. Through their interactions with others, he and the members of his clique exhibited their support for co-curricular activities. When I asked Mr. Zack to give the names of the people with whom he enjoyed socializing at Truman, he gave twenty-seven names. Most of his friends were involved with some aspect of coaching. Mr. Zack had a good deal of respect for the athletic director and often interacted with the other coaches during his breaks at Truman. That these linkages went beyond teachers within the social studies department was a detail that helped to distinguish the informal role expectations of one clique from the other: A teacher's endorsement of community values influenced social relations with the faculty in general. Theoretically, both Coaches and Academics could socialize with a variety of people while at work. The Coaches, unlike the Academics, did this, even though they had no more time for this socializing than the Academics. Coaches rarely expressed criticism about the community of Rillton and believed that participation in co-curricular activities, especially athletics, was important to high school teaching.

There was no force applied to join either clique, but achievement of status as a sustained member depended upon allegiance to the prevailing belief systems of the particular clique. When the social studies department held its weekly meetings, members filed into the chairperson's classroom singly or in groups of two or three. They took seats on different sides of the room, among other members of their clique, expressing support for their respective group, making it clear that Academics and Coaches held different views of the teacher's world. At times the informal seating arrangement served a more direct purpose, allowing members on either side to engage in internal repartee.

Playing Ball, Huddling, and Working the Shit Detail

The teachers in the Coach clique relied upon a variety of informal coping strategies and teaching methods for expressing their commitment to Rillton's expectations and fulfilling their dual role, of which *playing ball, huddling,* and *working the shit detail* were typical examples.

Playing ball, that is, athletic coaching, was supportive or professional in some ways and non-supportive or unprofessional in other ways. From the viewpoint of the Coaches, at least, it provided relief from what they called "an unworkable situation." From the Academics' viewpoint, playing ball was a compromise of principles because the practice of teaching social studies had too much in common with the management of athletic events. The Coaches regularly signed on to coach baseball, basketball, football, track, and wrestling. To look at the matter in a positive light, each of these teachers had considerable skill with organized games, and they enjoyed supervising their students in competitive sports. More importantly, coaching gave these teachers the opportunity to remain active and skilled in a sport they enjoyed playing. Since all of the Coaches lived in or very near the town of Rillton, commuting to and from school did not take up much time. When the team's practice was over, it was only a short drive or walk to their homes.

However, involvement with athletics also influenced what Coaches did in their classrooms. These teachers made conscious decisions at times to use methods that were unsuitable for teaching. For instance, the Coaches used materials and activities in their classes that they had developed for their co-curricular roles, some of which had little or nothing to do with social studies. As an example, Clifford Harris, the baseball coach, would use class time in the spring to demonstrate the calisthenics he believed best for baseball. Also, since there was only so much time available for preparation to work in both spheres of activity, it was inevitable that one activity would receive less attention than the other. "What's a teacher going to do?" Calvin Miller asked rhetorically. "I was up until 1:00 A.M. because of the game. There was no time to prepare for my first class this morning." The teachers' decision to conduct themselves in an unprofessional manner stemmed from the pressure they felt to fulfill the separate roles of social studies specialist and director of co-curricular activity.

When their respective athletic seasons were in full swing, the Coaches fixed their attention largely on developing strategies for competing with other teams. Between classes, during lunch, and after school these teachers concentrated on making game plans. Sometimes the Coach worked alone; at other times a group of Coaches would consult with one another about the best strategies. This concentration on athletic competition often conflicted with time needed for preparation to teach. One solution to the problem was extensive use of audiovisual materials. Another solution was to report highlights of the latest "fight" to students during class time.

The Academics held such teaching methods in low regard. In a show of resistance to the emphasis on co-curricular activities, members of the Academic clique ridiculed the Coaches for offering poor lectures during their particular athletic seasons. Sometime this ridiculing was done with the students. For example,

Anthony Finley once took bets with his class about when Calvin Miller, an assistant football coach (in the neighboring room), would stop showing videotapes of the games—at the end of the season, before the season ended, or some time after the last game. Mr. Finley was betting on the day after the end of the football season. He won. According to Mr. Finley, when the clock marked time for the Coach's class to begin and they heard no video from Mr. Miller's room, his own class "roared."

While administrators did not fully approve of the practices included under playing ball, they accepted them, because, they said, it was "hard to get good coaches" and the people of Rillton wanted to "see their team fighting." The administrators' policy of looking the other way in such instances emphasized the point that, for Coaches at least, one could literally play ball in the classroom as well as in the gym and on the playing fields. Looked at from the standpoint of teaching duties, a Coach could detract somewhat from the expected treatment of social studies curriculum during the season. This was as far as Truman's administrators would go in rewarding teachers for their co-curricular roles through adjustment of their work schedules.

This routine of playing ball illustrates the reflective process through which some teachers developed and acted upon their idea of teaching. The Coaches' teaching activity was a response to work conditions and to their own perceptions of the possibilities and the limits of their performance in the dual work role. Despite a tendency to use teaching materials and methods that were unsuitable for the social studies curriculum, there was congruity between their formal and informal role expectations. The informal group was the social agency that served both as a source for new ideas about one's practice in either teaching or coaching and as a source for moral support in regard to one's personal choice to engage in professional or unprofessional conduct.

Huddling was a related coping strategy that was common to the Coaches (cf. Schrank, 1978). This was a means the teachers used to solve a problem. During breaks from teaching, such as the lunch period, the Coaches frequently came together to discuss issues and problems, such as disciplining students, teaching a required subject, physical recreation for teachers, and so on. Often joined by other teachers who had commitments to athletic activities, they would also hold lively discussions about news of sports activities at all levels—local, regional, state, national, and international—and argue the pros and cons of equipment, sports records, and strategies. Regarding the latter, they would plan strategies for their teams and debate the effectiveness of one or another proposed alternative.

When huddling, it often happened that someone would recall that another teacher—one more experienced and respected—had set a precedent for solving the problem, and they would discuss its implications in the present situation. During one huddle, for example, Craig Zack, in referring to a conflict between himself and one of his students, said:

> I view it like one of my heroes, Curtis Jasper [a recently retired veteran of thirty-five years]. He believed that in the classroom as in the field, you gain in confidence in yourself through the mistakes you make. I know that I will make some more, but I'll work out an answer like Curtis did when the time comes.

Mr. Zack was using the huddle to pass on to his colleagues what he thought was an important lesson from an older and wiser teacher. In this way the huddle was a coaching session for the teachers themselves. The Coaches resolved problems that developed in the classroom through a process similar to that used on the playing fields—huddling. They met with other teachers during lunch periods, between classes, and after school to discuss accomplishments or mistakes they made and to "work out an answer." The problems encountered in both areas—classroom and gym—were serious concerns for the teachers. Arriving at solutions through huddling was an important informal role expectation. It provided a means for coping with the demands of teaching that were specific to those who taught social studies and coached in the co-curricular activities. By sharing their ideas, stories, and jokes in the huddles, the Coaches engaged in a process of reflective thinking about their practice of teaching.

It was in the huddle that these teachers gave one another ideas and support for the teaching methods and materials they used when their particular sport was in season. They knew that there was little or no relation between the videotape of a recent game and the current topic for the social studies curriculum. They believed that reliance on a film series, such as Alistair Cooke's *America*, would expose their students to American history, but they were also aware that such instruction was poor because it allowed little or no time for discussion. They used the time when films were showing to correct homework and exams and, occasionally, to catch up on sleep.

Many people—students, teachers, administrators, and parents—knew that a Coach's teaching was poor when the game was in season. The library records of requests for audiovisual materials verified that the Coaches made heavy use of them. In the discussion of the previous topic, playing ball, I noted that the authorities for the school expressed a willingness to "look the other way" when the team was playing. On one occasion the superintendent and high school principal demonstrated their complicity while standing outside of Calvin Miller's classroom, looking through the doorway at a videotape of a recent football game that was playing for the students. In response to my question about what was going on in the classroom, the principal reminded me that "good coaches are hard to come by." The supervisors agreed that Calvin Miller could do good work in either activity, coaching or teaching. However, evidence such as this, indicating that the dual role had an adverse effect on teaching the social studies curriculum, was not enough to convince administrators of a need to restructure the teacher's work to provide relief.

It was commonly agreed by Coaches that those in the Academic clique were good teachers—they were steeped in economic, political, and social theory and could teach well. This belief helped explain why certain Academics taught such courses to seniors, and it also explained the authority structure in the Academic clique. However, some of the Coaches had been teaching other required senior-level courses for many years, a circumstance that the Academics hoped and fought to change. In the opinion of Academics, a teacher's assignment to a low-level social studies course indicated that he or she was a "rotten teacher." On the one hand, this meant that the teacher had a low level of competence with subject matter. On the other hand, the Coaches were willing to embrace the task because they knew that sophomore and low-level students were less likely to complain about methods and materials for instruction. Although the assignment to teach low-level sophomores was most common among Coaches and aspirers in the Academic clique, teachers in both cliques received such assignments and all of them referred to it as "being given the shit detail."

While many of those in the Coach clique received assignments to teach low-level sophomore courses, not all who had the assignment were ineffective teachers. The Coaches had evolved a response to the situation that was protective. Those who were assigned to teach such courses were aware of the negative stereotype, yet they took the matter seriously and assumed a protectionist point of view. Craig Zack explained what he did for a low-level student. It was representative of what others did.

> I got a guy in my class this year who had three independent
> studies last year, because nobody wanted him. I have
> teachers come up to me and say: "You mean you have _____
> in your class? How do you put up with him?" There are
> teachers who do not want him. I am able to handle it because
> I have been down that road before. And my communication
> with his parents was important. I pointed out to them that he
> could do C-level work or better. Right now he's really work-
> ing and his parents are impressed.

Craig Zack's reason for working the shit detail was to protect students from "dropping out of school and getting into trouble with the law." He and the other members of the Coach clique believed that if they did not show some concern for these students, then nobody would. As Clifford Harris explained, "Some of these kids come from bad family situations. They need somebody to show them a different way of living." Unlike the Academics, who placed a high value on scholarly study, the Coaches emphasized knowing the student.

For teachers like Mr. Zack, redefining the situation known as *working the shit detail* was a pragmatic response to an exigency of public high school teaching. Doing so meant that one put emphasis upon affecting good behavior among students, presenting structured subject matter and carefully planned lessons during the off-season, and using questionable teaching practices with discretion when the game was in season. On the face of it, the Coaches' teaching conduct may seem to be poor or ill advised. Upon taking a closer look, their handling of the situation was a subtle effort to reconcile the conflicting demands for high levels of performance in both teaching and co-curricular activity. As a small group, the Coaches had developed a repertoire of beliefs and activities for teaching that allowed them to get the job done and to satisfy, at least minimally, the expectations from their supervisors and the community of Rillton.

What Coaches did in the name of working the shit detail was similar to what Cusick (1983) reports about teachers in Factory

High: "Not only does the teacher have to maintain the framework of decent personal relations, he or she has to pull the deviating students into some cohesiveness and at the same time keep articulating the experience" (p. 66). Social studies teachers at Truman who had low-level students in their classes developed an approach to teaching that emphasized the personal interests of individuals and the social interests of high school students in general. Craig Zack summed it up with, "We are concerned with kids." They expressed their concern openly to parents in their coaching of teams in the gym and on the playing field; it was also evident in their instruction of low-level students in their classrooms.

Craig Zack explained his philosophy of teaching as follows:

> I want to know how we can tune more of these kids into this thing called Truman High School or Rillton. I look upon teachers as leaders in the community. Our number one concern is kids. That's why I'm in it. In one case baseball, in another history. I think kids have a higher respect for you if they know you are a person who has a concern for them that isn't just in the classroom.

Mr. Zack strongly believed that all students, but especially sophomores, needed constant exposure to proper adult role models, careful guidance in making decisions, and "consistency" in their academic and social life. In his opinion, the high incidence of divorce in the area, absence of parents in the homes due to the family's need for a double income, and availability and widespread use of drugs in the high school and community set adolescents up for easy slippage into "a losing situation." The subject matter he (and the others) presented in the classroom and his involvement with co-curricular activities reflected this concern. For example, he would take time out during class to talk about problems for adolescents, such as drug abuse, alcoholism, and theft. One day when the administration hastily added to the schedule a guest speaker who would be addressing these problems, Craig Zack cancelled his class and required that his students attend.

However, the Coaches, and especially Craig Zack, were very well aware that their efforts to interrelate academic and co-curricular interests were sometimes rebuffed and at other times not recognized by the administration. In regard to the behaviors I call "playing ball" and "huddling," there is a rather obvious relationship to the athletic program. When these teachers said they were "working the shit detail," they went beyond the co-curricular assignment. In this way they were accepting responsibility for one of the least popular assignments among social studies teachers— working with sophomore-level classes or low-level students. The Coaches' acceptance and transformation of the shit detail demonstrates their dependence on the informal group and the adaptive or coping behaviors it produced.

Teachers in both cliques told me that the school authorities failed to recognize and reward self-expression that was personal, intentional, and creative. "No one gives a shit," Alan Silvius said. "Administrators give better evaluations to teachers who have been here longer. They could care less about what I did," Amy Bentley said. Teachers like Mr. Silvius, Ms. Bentley, and Mr. Zack wanted the institution to take into account the fact that teachers as well as students needed to grow through the process of schooling. Because he believed independent study and professional association were important to his work as a teacher, he found time for these while at work and, more often, at home. Frustrated that the institution avoided the problem of malaise issuing from the dual role expectation for teachers, the Academics and Coaches created outlets for self-expression through informal group activity.

The teachers' primary responsibility was to hold classes in their rooms. They did this for five periods per day. In addition to time for teaching, they had assignments for preparation, lunch, study hall supervision, and hallway monitoring. The lunch break was the only period on the schedule that allowed teachers to associate freely. However, there were two shifts for lunch, which meant that the teachers had limits placed on their collegial relations at this time also.

Given the tight schedule of work, the time available to teachers for independent study or professional association with colleagues was minimal and its use was a matter of personal choice. Teachers appreciated these times but believed they were of little value from the standpoint of the institution. "I think of all the workshops, seminars, publications, and fellowships that I have done; it is conceivable that none of this would make any difference in my career," Amy Bentley explained. Teachers like Amy Bentley maintained an interest in professional growth despite the fact that the school's formal organization neither recognized nor rewarded it. But they felt frustration.

These men and women believed the administration muted (unintentionally) personal and professional growth by adhering to traditional conceptions of work in schools. In their opinion the emphasis placed upon policies dealing with maintenance of attendance, discipline, and co-curricular activities interfered with their teaching role. "Why do I have to watch these hallways?" Andy Abraham said. "There are a hundred other things that are more important to improving my courses." Alfred Moore explained that if there were teachers who believed this was an important part of their work, then they should be the ones who do it. The teachers in the Academic clique viewed this policy as a drain because it took attention away from the academic program and, in particular, from the teachers' need for a structure of work that facilitated professional growth.

Black Humor, Playing the Game, and Pimping

Like their blue-collar cousins, the social studies teachers knew how to have fun on the job (cf. LeMasters, 1975; Schrank, 1978). The men in the Academic clique, in particular, engaged in coping mechanisms called *black humor, playing the game,* and *pimping.* Whether because of or in spite of frustrations associated with the structure of work at Truman, these teachers developed forms of horseplay to express autonomy and creativity in the workplace. Some forms of playful activity allowed them to find relief and opportunity for personal expression through humor, but the particular variety was an unconventional response to the workplace.

Black humor is the tendency to regard as humorous what most people would perceive to be morbid or sad. A number of contemporary American novelists write in this genre. Two of the more well known are Joseph Heller and Kurt Vonnegut, Jr. Members of the Academic clique took pleasure in responding to situations with black humor, and sometimes it did not matter to them who was in their audience.

The following are representative examples of this activity.

At 3:30 P.M. on March 30, 1981, one of the teachers walked into a classroom and said, "Boy, am I having a hard time keeping from laughing. At one point in the hallway I couldn't control it any longer and I busted out laughing in front of

some students. I just had to tell them. They wanted to know
what I thought was so funny. So I did. I said, 'The assassination of President Reagan.'"

It was on this date that John Hinkley made an assassination
attempt, but succeeded only in wounding the president and three
of his aides. At 2:30 P.M. the principal had made an announcement
on the public address system informing the whole school of the
event and the condition of the injured. To conclude, the principal
said, "No matter what our political preferences are, this is a very
tragic and deplorable act." The teacher's response in the hallway
was an expression of black humor addressed to the students and to
the principal.

The second example concerns a time when the social studies
department members were waiting to begin one of their meetings.
The brief situation unfolded as follows:

> One of those in the Academic clique told the group of
> teachers gathered in the classroom that the way to get rid of
> the slums is to kill the Pope. A teacher who was seeking
> membership in the Academic clique made an obvious nod of
> assent. At the same time, a teacher in the Coach clique said
> to the one who had spoken: "If you did as much for the world
> as the Pope, it would be a better place to live."

Those who were not members of the Academic clique sometimes
took offense at what the Academics considered humorous. Use of
black humor by the Academics was a distinguishing characteristic and a coping strategy that, like others discussed in this book,
enhanced clique solidarity.

On the face of it, the various ways in which the Academics
engaged in black humor may seem absurd. However, black humor
provided teachers in the Academic clique with a form of comic
relief that they found satisfying. Provision of comic relief was one
of the reasons why teachers in the Academic clique stayed on at
Truman.

Another form of comic relief engaged in by the Academics was
playing the game. In its simplest sense, a game is an activity
engaged in for diversion or amusement. The ethos of the Academic
clique included games with a twofold objective: those that gave
players immediate satisfaction and those whose long-range objective was to secure strategic control over the social studies depart-

ment. *Playing the game* relieved those teachers of the tedium involved in their work and the frustrations associated with a work structure that isolated teachers from one another. Playing the game involved jokes spontaneously developed by members of the Academic clique. Belonging to this clique included the informal role expectation that one would help to lighten things up. By itself, this activity illustrates how the Academics made their job more bearable. The character of this play helps explain the conflict over formal role expectations among teachers in the two cliques, the school authorities, and the community of Rillton.

One of the games played for immediate satisfaction involved word play on the names of administrators. For example, a teacher who had received a reprimand for improper conduct by the assistant principal, whose name was Vincent Holmes, would say to another member of the clique that he had been "Vinced." Academics used the same expression whenever this assistant principal was observing one of them for evaluation of their teaching performance. "Silvius is being Vinced today," Arnold Wilkes told Andy Abraham during class-change time. This statement carried both humor and a signal that the assistant principals had started their annual evaluations of teachers. Abraham and Wilkes could expect the assistant principal to visit their classrooms at any time soon. The game relieved teachers of the tension and frustration associated with an evaluation process that they believed was inappropriate.

The teachers' frustration grew out of the distance they perceived between themselves and administrators and the manner in which some administrators carried out their duties. I asked Alan Silvius to comment on his experience with the evaluation. He said:

> Let me tell you what Holmes did to me once at the old building. I was lecturing one day and he came bursting through the door, slammed it shut, and walked straight back to a desk in the rear of the room. I felt like slapping him in the face. Instead, I had my kids look over their notes for ten minutes while I calmed down. Boy, was I mad.

The example provided by Mr. Silvius indicates that at least one administrator, Vincent Holmes, used the evaluation of teachers as a form of harassment. Other examples from teachers showed less drama and less interference from the administrators, but no more concern for providing teachers with guidance in their professional work role. Generally speaking, in the opinion of teachers, how administrators evaluated teachers had less to do with the teacher's classroom performance than with the number of years he or she had taught in the district.

In playing the game, the emphatic "put down" was one of a variety of strategies used by teachers. It was common for these teachers to put down administrators in front of students. In one instance two teachers were discussing Vincent Holmes in a class-room while a student was sitting a few feet away. During their conversation, one of the teachers said loudly: "Holmes is a *dumb* shit."

Generally speaking, the Academic clique had little apprecia-tion for administrators, resented surprise visits for evaluation of their work, and believed that they could conduct themselves re-sponsibly throughout the year without them. When interacting with administrators on an informal or a formal basis, the Academ-ics played the game privately. Art Finley exhibited his skill at the private manner of playing the game in the following story:

> We were waiting for a ride in the lobby. I didn't see him
> [Vincent Holmes] there at first; he's kind of like a wallflower.
> He saw us and then we saw him. It was 3:50 P.M. He looked
> at his watch and said: "You can go now." We said: "Thanks."
> His [comment] was in jest, not pricky. We said: "Thanks a lot
> (you son of a bitch)." He was trying to make peace with that
> statement and I didn't want to come across like him. He
> usually treats teachers like an SOB would.

When the teachers were attending some event they disliked, the private version of the game was a means of entertainment for them. They almost always resorted to this means of gaining relief during meetings with administrators. They would share their private exploits with one another while riding home after work. It was a feature of the belief system developed by the Academics that assured members of mutual support and a spirit of togetherness.

I noticed this spirit of togetherness periodically while riding in the car pool and during other clique activities. When somebody told of a secret escape (see Chapter 5) or pimping (see below), Andy Abraham would remind the others that I was an outsider and say to them, "You better be careful what you say, because he's [nodding at me] writing all of this down."

Mutually supportive activity is common in many workplaces. Schrank (1978), for example, reports about the spirit of togetherness among furniture factory workers. One of the workers in the factory inducted Schrank into the informal group with, "Look kid, the boss always wants more and he doesn't give a shit if we die giving it to him, so we agree on how much we are going to give him—no more, no less." In other words, the worker should do what benefits other workers and not simply please the boss. Schrank's point is that the informal group generates the norms that are important to a worker's continuance on the job.

The social studies teachers looked upon school administrators in much the same way that Schrank's furniture factory workers looked upon the boss. While I was interviewing Art Heidman on this topic in the lounge, he picked up from the table a small plastic figure of a basketball player poised to make a shot. "I'd like to break this," he said while turning it over in his hand. "That's what I think about the setup." In his opinion, to function efficiently, the administration needed teachers who were willing followers. If you wanted to please the boss, sign up for co-curricular activities and "be a Coach" in the hallways. These were things that Coaches did.

A game played by the male Academics involved female students. A teacher would select the most outstanding girl in class for the day based upon revealing dress, cleavage, general good looks, and so on, and give her a book to deliver to one of the others in the clique during class-change time as a "little present." To give the game a new twist, a teacher sent the fattest and ugliest girl he had on the same kind of errand. Having a "sexy" girl suddenly show up at the door before class subverted the administration's desire to manage the work of teachers and provided teachers with an instant of relief from ongoing events planned for the conventionally organized school day. Playing this puerile game may have stemmed from extensive time spent with adolescents. It may also have been a mechanism devised by teachers to cope with discontinuities in the two role expectations.

In the following memo Truman's administration made clear its position regarding management of events in the high school. The document is a representative sample of forms of communication sent from the administrators to the teachers.

DATE: September 15, 1980
  TO: All Teaching Staff and Hall Aides
FROM: Administration
  RE: Assembly Procedure & Assignments

Assembly attendance is required of ALL students
and teachers. Some teachers will be assigned as door monitors and others will be assigned to sit among the students.
Teachers who are not assigned to specific duties are expected
to disperse themselves among the students on the bleachers.
Teachers are not to sit in pairs or teacher groups, or stand
along the walls or bleachers. Dismissal will be by the P.A.,
by zones. Attached is a map outlining the zones. When your
zone is called over the P.A., you are to direct your students to
the field house bleachers. Books go with students to the field
house, and students are not to go to their lockers. You are expected to help with the directing of students to the bleachers
as you take your seat. Do not permit any students to leave
the building unless they have a utility slip from the office.
After the students have moved to the gymnasium, Aides and
Hall Monitors are to check the rest rooms for stragglers and
move them to the field house.

With a little imagination, one gets the impression that these are
instructions for driving cattle through a stockyard. The instructions are explicit and call for literal interpretation. Teachers perceived the message as an insult to their intelligence.

As we were taking our seats during one assembly, Anthony
Finley said of his assignment, "This is an example of the petty and
nitpicky things that administrators do to teachers." During assemblies, one could not sit with a colleague, nor could a group of
teachers sit together. Teachers had assigned seats for the purpose
of maintaining order among students. As we left the field house,
teachers walked alongside the students with whom they had been
sitting. If teachers spoke at all, it was idle conversation to students
near them. Now and then one would reprimand a student for
misbehavior.

From the teachers' point of view, school authorities placed
undue emphasis on order and in doing so created policies that
denied teachers an opportunity for adult socialization on a professional basis while on the job. The teachers saw this external form
of control as indicative of policies that affected their work in
school in general. As a result, the teachers believed the administration slighted their needs for personal and professional growth.
The practical jokes on the job, such as those invented by the
Academics, explain how they found relief through inappropriate
adolescent behavior.

Cusick (1983) argues that the maintenance of order forms the basis of a high school curriculum. Teachers in the schools he studied had one obligation: "Get along with kids." Good teaching meant keeping students "in a moderate state of order, maintain some cordial relations with them, and not send for administrative assistance" (p. 60). Teachers in the schools Cusick studied developed "idiosyncratic approaches." Frustrated about the isolation from other adults and angry about alleged or perceived insults from administrators, teachers at Truman created amenities through informal group strategies that helped them cope with disappointing features of the institution. Playing the game with female students was but one example of how teachers in the Academic clique acted like their teenage students while on the job at Truman High.

The social studies teachers sometimes played the game by getting satisfaction at the expense of colleagues. While both teacher groups had established certain subject matter as exclusive preserves, the Academics were striving continuously to gain control of the department. The strategies they used were largely subversive. During one department meeting on curriculum planning, the Academics attempted to cut short the discussion of a so-called "tentative proposal" for changing course descriptions and tried to trick Coaches into signing their names, showing agreement. Clayton Samuels became suspicious of the other side's motives and said, "You're not going to weigh all of this argument and take it back to the [district] committee. You haven't listened to a single word we've said in here today." Indeed, the Academics were not planning to report to their district committee, but to the central office administrator whose verbal endorsement they had garnered secretly. At the end of the meeting Art Heidman passed out sheets of paper for everyone's signature and, when the Coaches had all left, said to me, "I can't wait to see their signatures on those papers." If a majority of department members signed, then certain required courses taught only by Coaches would become electives. A reduction of required courses taught by Coaches meant more junior and senior level students in the Academics' classes.

Finally, in a sporting activity with their students, members of the Academic clique ridiculed teachers for whom they had no respect. Coaches were usually the objects of their ridicule. Since Coaches were involved in co-curricular activities, especially athletics, stereotyping of the athlete as a jock or macho man was common. The Academic clique had two reasons for stereotyping

Coaches as they did. One reason was to draw attention to differences in techniques of handling behavior problems in the school. Academics tended to rely on logical argument and persuasion, while Coaches tended to rely more heavily on physical force or the threat of it. Another reason for stereotyping Coaches was to gain support from students for the subject-matter orientation of the Academic clique. Members of the Academic clique were able to alleviate some of their frustration concerning the institution's demand for work in both the academic program and the co-curricular activities by playing the game against their colleagues.

To embarrass or rankle someone through a verbal exchange was a manner of interacting with colleagues that the Academics themselves referred to as *pimping*. It was done for fun as a practical joke with friends; for those who were not friends, it was done to abuse them. Included in these two classes of people were teachers, administrators, students, and parents. For example, if two teachers who were friends met by chance in the school hallway, the one might greet the other with, "Hi, you son of a bitch." To this the other might respond with, "You prick." Another common way of pimping someone in fun was to flash "the finger." The same gesture might be returned by the other teacher.

An example of the way pimping was used for abuse occurred during a social studies department meeting when a central office administrator was giving a presentation to the teachers. Art Heidman had done the pimping and explained the event in the following way:

> During his presentation there were pauses of fifteen to
> twenty minutes. Can you believe it? He had a bulletin board
> and he had written drivel on some cards and some posters
> like: skills, values, content, and concepts. And when he
> pointed to it, I looked at Arnold and laughed like it was
> something he [Arnold] was impressed with. We made fun of
> his [the administrator's] presentation. It was stupid. I'd have
> been embarrassed to present it to one of my classes. He was
> clearly uncomfortable and out of his element.

When animosity characterized the relationship between individuals or groups who were meeting, pimping was done to destroy something in the other.

Pimping was an overt expression of the teachers' frustration with isolation from colleagues and continual association with adolescents. As with each of the previous strategies of Academics, it served the teachers first and the educational program second, if at all. Whether done as a practical joke with friends or to abuse authority figures and Coaches, pimping offered the men in the Academic clique a chance to have fun while enduring what they believed were undesirable or dehumanizing aspects of teaching. These teachers felt frustration with a work structure that offered minimum opportunities for teachers to associate freely with adults while on the job, and they believed the administration abused or discounted the need for professional supervision. From the standpoint of the Academics, Truman failed to take into account fully the needs of the people who worked there as teachers.

Summary

Employment at the high school and experiences common to social studies teachers determined to a great extent the opportunities that a teacher had for collegial relationships at Truman High. The Academic and Coach cliques arose out of the voluntary association of sixteen teachers who had joined the faculty over a twenty-year period. Individual members helped shape the peculiar behaviors that sustained the cliques over this time.

Academics and Coaches believed that the policies adopted by authorities for the school interfered with a teacher's responsibilities for educating high school students. Different individuals from each clique pointed out that the structure of work and the dual role expectation from Rillton and administrators were aspects of the job that drained them of energy. The day-to-day contact with students gave teachers an intimate acquaintance with problems peculiar to educating youth at Truman High. However, the administrators and school board members made decisions that affected the education program in important ways, and these officials had no direct involvement with classroom instruction. The administration's reliance upon a hierarchical but incongruous design for supervision contributed to the emergence of a faculty subculture that promoted the interests of teachers. Frequently the teachers' interests concerned their intergroup struggle instead of the aims of the institution.

The teaching profession is not the only one in which people will form themselves into cliques; nor do all small, informal groups come into rivalry with one another to establish discordant role expectations. The structure of work in school settings minimizes contact between teachers while they are working. Despite the tightness of the structure, the two cliques in the social studies department at Truman High formed themselves and supported their members in one of two competing definitions of the teacher's role. Whether one was a Coach or an Academic, the teacher enjoyed the benefits of the informal group. These faculty subcultures created functional, albeit sometimes prankish, behavior that increased an individual's chances of surviving through the days, weeks, and years on the job. Each set of activities had potential for supporting and detracting from the aims of the high school. Too often, these activities supported a role that was unsuitable for the teacher. In effect, the teachers' activity tended to sanction a workplace mentality at Truman that included a mischievous desire to survive on the job.

CHAPTER 4

The Routine

One Monday morning I walked into Andy Abraham's first-period class as his students were entering. He was expecting me and immediately asked, "Do you really want to know what it's like to be a teacher?" I said, "Yes, I do." He continued, "Then, watch this closely." He was standing at the podium with his record book and a pad of paper for reporting students who were absent or tardy from class. To verify attendance, he placed a checkmark in his record book for each student who was present. After the second bell rang announcing the start of class, he made a list of students who were absent or tardy and attached this list with a metal clip to the doorjamb. About fifteen minutes later a student would come down the hall, pick up these slips of paper from every teacher's door, and prepare a report for the principal.

There was nothing particularly exciting about this activity. It was an orderly and systematic procedure that he completed at least five times each day. Why did Andy Abraham attach importance to it? There was an uncommon smoothness to his action. The simple, technical procedure seemed to be second nature for him. Although he was finessing now for a small audience, it was clearly a well-established habit. "If you can do this," Andy Abraham said to me and some students in the front row, "then *you* can be a teacher, too." I asked him if he was joking. He continued:

> Not really. You've got to have a routine for all of these details or else they will bury you. The bell just rang about five minutes ago, and I have not started class yet. It's going to ring again in about forty minutes, and I have to assign homework, check homework, give a lecture, answer questions—if there are any—pass out materials, and deal with whatever *else*

happens. This goes on five times a day. Teachers have got to have routines and have them down cold, or they're doomed.

With that said, Mr. Abraham told his students to take out their notebooks. He wanted to see the homework they had done over the previous weekend. The class period was under way, he was into his next routine, and he did not want to fall further behind schedule.

Unless there was a special event scheduled for the day, the teachers had exactly forty-seven minutes to complete their work for each class. From the first bell of the day to the start of the first class, students had only three minutes to get to their classrooms. Class-change times after the first period of the day also consisted of three hectic minutes. At these times the hallways filled with students rushing noisily, sometimes wildly, to lockers, restrooms, and classrooms. The administration required teachers to stand at their doors during class-change times to monitor the activity of students in the hallway. Seldom would all of the students be in class in time for the next bell announcing the start of classes.

Taking attendance occupied a particularly important place among the many routines in the work life of the teacher. Failure to maintain the routine or use it to advantage could lead to serious trouble. The administration relied upon this requirement to keep a record of attendance on students and to keep tabs on teachers. Students were quick to spot a teacher's mistake in any routine; they would use the situation to misbehave.

The teachers' skill in routines was a necessary and habitual aspect of their formal work role. Nothing should interrupt the teacher during the routine. Teachers believed that they could not complete their work without the routines and were aware that the conduct of the ceremonial activity itself provided a modicum of relief from their work schedule and the student activities. Sometimes the teachers' facility with routines saved them and their students from embarrassment or ruin. However, an excessive, unselfconscious use of routines indicated that a teacher had lost interest in the job and had little or no respect for others, especially students.

I had made arrangements to hitch a ride to Idolville that evening with Andy Abraham's car pool and stay the night with Anthony Finley and his family. The car pool, I found, offered the rider more than a convenient and less expensive mode of travel to and from work. The teachers used the ride home with colleagues as an opportunity to express private thoughts and rid themselves of workday frustrations. Strategies for coping with the work routines, including sparring with administrators and dealing with the students' typically adolescent behavior, was a recurrent theme. Clifford Geertz (1983) aptly defined this behavior as "reiterated form, staged and acted by its own audience." In effect, the teachers' ride home was a little ritual of self-esteem against the ever-present likelihood of disrepute (see Waller, 1932).

The Ride Home

We left Truman High School promptly at 3:45 P.M. and went to the parking lot. Andy Abraham was driving. Since I was an extra rider and it was a small car, I asked where he wanted me to sit. Art Heidman said, "In there. In the back." He was pointing to the center position over the hump. I climbed in the back with Alan Silvius and Art Heidman, while Anthony Finley and Alfred Moore sat up front with Mr. Abraham. The car had just left the lot when Art Heidman exclaimed, "The nerve of that student!" The others looked at him and shook their heads, as if they understood. "What is it this time?" Alan Silvius asked. Art Heidman continued.

You are not going to believe this. Remember Rick? Well, I'm doing the colonial era in my American history classes. I'd been talking about the lives of the Pilgrims and decided to read a little from William Bradford's book, *Of Plymouth Plantation*. I had this lecture all worked out and I was getting excited and looking forward to a discussion, when somebody interrupts me and says: "Is that all they did is work and pray?" I should have stopped right there.

No. Instead, I turned to the section in the book on the Maypole affair and told them that these people were human, too. I started to read the account. When I got to the part about the frisking around, Rick, in the back of the room, cuts a fart. Dammit all anyway. The whole class breaks out in laughter, except for a few people up front. I just turned around to the board and swore up and down to myself. What in the hell are you going to do?

No one in the car pool was laughing. They were staring out of the windows at the countryside that was passing them by. Andy Abraham looked into the rearview mirror at Art Heidman and said: "You asked for it. You tried something different."

There was a long period of silence. Then Alan Silvius spoke. The tone of his voice was uncheerful and the statement was matter-of-fact. He said:

> I had a girl in my class last year who would wait for the per-
> fect moment in one of my lectures, just like this guy, Rick.
> I'd be ready to make a point and she'd flash her breast at
> me. At first I tried to ignore it. You know. Maybe she's
> scratching herself. Then, I talked with her. That did no good
> either. I got frustrated, so I went down to Guidance and
> Counseling. They said they'd try to do something for me. The
> whole term it was like that.

Anthony Finley told the group that he had overheard Clayton Samuels talking in the lounge about the activity of this particular girl in one of his classes. Samuels had found a solution to the problem by using the system. He documented every instance of the girl's inappropriate behavior, gave the evidence to the Guidance Office, and had them remove the girl from his class for disorderly conduct. Anthony Finley concluded his story with this refrain, "That's no solution, but it's just about the only thing you can do about it."

The teachers traded other stories about the rude or vulgar activity they witnessed from students. Sometimes the students' activity was belligerent as well as embarrassing. For example, Anthony Finley told about a student who was obese and had a repulsive odor. Other students in the class resented sitting near him. When Mr. Finley attempted to give this student some suggestions privately about how to deal with his personal health and hygiene, the student told him to "go fuck off." After that, the student would belch and fart during class, apparently attempting to provoke, and always embarrassing, Mr. Finley in front of the other students. In the car pool, though, there was always someone who had a consoling phrase to offset the teachers' inevitable loss of self-esteem.

There also were times when a personal or family tragedy affected everyone in the classroom. For instance, Alfred Moore told about the return to his class of a student whose sister had been killed in a car accident. He explained his reliance on the routines of teaching with, "You have to show some genuine concern for the student in a situation like that, but you also have to go on because the students expect you to and they need it to cope. But it ain't easy."

More often, however, the classroom behavior of students was what these teachers called a "silly or emotional response." For example, Alfred Moore recalled a time during one of his lectures when something told him that the room was too quiet. At that very moment, unknown to Mr. Moore, a student in the back of the room was attempting to open a bag of M and M's. The bag would not tear open, so the student applied more pressure until it burst, spreading its contents throughout the room. In a second, Mr. Moore lost any sense of dramatic build-up that he might have developed in relation to his topic. "It is important that a teacher not become rattled by the silly little things that kids do," he said, "otherwise you cannot complete the simplest routine."

While investigating the world of high school students, Philip Cusick (1973) described what he came to know about teachers. In doing so he selected routinization to describe one important "reinforcer" of school organization. "There are few differences," Cusick (1973) observed, "in the way teachers plan their classes and present material" (p. 35). The effect on both students and teachers was that they would never be in doubt about where to go and when to be there. That Cusick took routine to be important for explaining activities expected of students by teachers is understandable, for he was largely concerned with student behavior.

Members of both cliques at Truman believed their job demanded a facile skill with routinizing the process of teaching. Their successful completion of a simple routine, like taking attendance, helped to keep them on schedule and to remain alert for deviant student behavior. If a teacher was successful with simple and supportive routines, there was a greater likelihood of success with more complex routines, like lecturing. On the downside, as Waller (1932) noted, "it is hard to see how loss of enthusiasm can be avoided; that is part of the fundamental difficulty of being a teacher, that one must go on doing things that have lost their appeal because one has done them so many times" (p. 226). The disruptions from students or from the administration may have been galling, but they were nonetheless stimulating exceptions to the ordinary flow of classroom activity. These teachers were aware that their daily use of formal and informal routines included self-conscious and unselfconscious applications and had potential for both positive and negative effects. The experienced teachers' deft handling of routines and ritual storytelling after work made their activities seem natural and hid the source of trouble.

These teachers wanted to provide their students with high-quality instruction in social studies, but they believed the policies of the school—chiefly, the placement of low-level students in their classes, coupled with the regimentation of the schedule—stymied their plans for work. While the teachers believed the school should serve all students, they had serious misgivings about policies having to do with enrollment and discipline. They also expressed concern about the manner in which school authorities made decisions that would affect their work. Teachers perceived the administration and the school board to be responding to the public demand for equal rights in education for all students, without fully considering the needs of teachers.

The teachers believed that if they were to respond to the needs of emotionally disturbed, learning-disabled, or mentally retarded students and also maintain high standards in academic programs and co-curricular areas, then institutional policies had to provide for their own professional needs in substantive ways (see Sykes, 1983). But from the teachers' point of view, school policies seemed to have more to do with respecting principles of efficient management than with respecting the professional concerns of the classroom teacher. The workplace mentality of social studies teachers at Truman High reflected, in part, a need for more involvement in decision making.

Clifford Harris gave an explanation that was representative of opinions held by other teachers in the social studies department:

> Nothing has prepared me for teaching slow learners in the high school. I have slow learners, emotionally disturbed kids, some who are mentally retarded, and the regular kids. They [administrators] don't give you release time to develop courses. The specialists don't know the subject matter that the kid is working on. They just help him do just what the task calls for, never questioning him as I would. It bothers me.
>
> I have seventeen or eighteen of those kids in here. The specialists have four or five in their classes. Now they can isolate those kids with emotional problems and deal with them effectively. How can you do that with so many? Christ, what a mess. Are we doing these kids an injustice?

Mr. Harris believed that the response of the school authorities to the public demand for equalization of educational opportunities overlooked the teachers' needs. The administration allowed officials in the Guidance Office to place students with exceptional educational needs in classes without serious attention to the impact on the work of teachers.

In addition to the problems posed by the special educational needs of some students, the teachers faced the challenges common to teaching all adolescents. Their approach to social studies instruction included trying new ideas and methods as well as relying on established content and routine activities. However, the teachers perceived the continual preparation of novel approaches for handling subject matter and the problems with students as a "drain" that led to a "collapse." The "silly" or "screwy" activity that they believed was typical of adolescents had wrecked many of their best efforts. Teachers in both cliques knew they could minimize the irksome or ruinous consequences that were always possible on the job by following tried-and-true routines. From the teachers' point of view, the conditions of work sanctioned routine, which fulfilled two of their significant needs: assurance that the job could be done and protection from the loss of self-esteem that accompanied a gamble with something new and different.

Research by Lortie (1975) and Maeroff (1988) shows that in the teaching career, aspects such as isolation from colleagues and limited involvement with institutional-level decision making tend to exacerbate uncertainty about one's capacity. Lortie (1975) argues that the longer one does the work of teaching, the worse are the effects: The uncertainty associated with the effects of one's work as a teacher contribute to "diffuse anxiety and painful self-doubt" (p. 161). The workplace culture of teachers may be partly responsible for these results, according to Lortie and Maeroff, for it stresses themes that are antithetical to adaptability, collegiality, and sharing. Teachers in turn stress these themes, but at Truman the definition of the teacher's role and activity occurred within small informal groups because there it served the interests peculiar to teachers.

Like teachers in other schools, these teachers developed instructional routines for recurrent situations. The routines, sustained by ritual storytelling, helped them last through the school year. Yet an uncritical use of routines was the mark of bad teaching, because it erroneously made unselfconscious teacher behavior into an ideal role expectation. When overused and when taken to the extreme, even the self-conscious use of a teaching routine could lead to unprofessional activity. These teachers wanted to guard themselves from the extremes and had worked out some means to do so in their informal groups. Their uncritical reliance on routine was a hidden effect of collegiality. *Lecturing and recitation* describes the instructional routine itself; *deadness versus vitality*, the conditions that derived from it; *the trap*, both attitudes toward controlling subject matter and techniques for controlling students.

Lecture and Recitation

There was a contradiction in the formal role expectation developed by the social studies teachers. They described themselves as subject-matter specialists who distinguished themselves from traditional teachers by using "different content and different methods of teaching." In the social studies classrooms, these teachers perceived themselves as involving students in discussions of contemporary issues instead of merely requiring them to listen to lectures or write answers to textbook questions. This perception of their methods was common among teachers in both cliques. However, it was more a description of what they were hoping for than what one actually found in either clique.

The wide range of student interests and academic abilities coupled with the capricious behavior of twenty to thirty different adolescents each hour for five hours a day encouraged teachers to use the routines of lecture and recitation. Craig Zack candidly explained the problem.

I feel guilty about having a class of just twenty-four students, made up of twenty who don't want to learn and four who do. You find yourself addressing the twenty, because they'll run away with the class otherwise. So, you are always trying to find a way where the twenty will allow you to teach a class.

The way involved *lecture and recitation*. Teachers believed that these routines were necessary, because the principal, counselors, and specialists had control over who was in class and for how long. These were small decisions made by various superordinates in the school, but, as Lortie (1975) notes, they influence the curriculum. According to Art Heidman, since the teacher had no choice but to "contend with those dirts and snobs assigned to the class," along with a few who wanted to be there, then one had to routinize teaching activities because that would get the job done.

For the majority of time that students were in social studies classes, they were listening to lectures or reciting from their notebooks. The typical example was as follows. The lecture usually began with a definition of a main term, such as *economic recession*. Then, in step-by-step fashion, the teacher put a "bare-bones outline" on the chalkboard, elaborating on each subdivision with its supporting details. "Here are the three things you should concentrate on," the teacher would say while writing on the board.

As the teacher did this, the students copied these words in their notebooks. Occasionally the teacher read from a primary source, cited support from assigned readings, or involved students in an exercise. When asking students to provide examples, the teacher often supplied them or modified what a student offered to such an extent that it became the teacher's own example. The teachers expected students to take notes throughout the lecture. However, despite the amount said by a teacher about a topic, the "bare-bones outline" usually became the students' lecture notes.

The teacher held a discussion session on the following day, checking the students' notebooks and having them recite the main points of the lecture. The following was typical of recitation sessions:

At the start of class Craig Zack reminded the students that he had lectured to them on "The Modern Problems of Work" during class on the previous day. After taking attendance, Mr. Zack announced: "We will get into a discussion of 'The Modern Problems of Work' today." At this time he moved into the aisles to look at notebooks and, as he did so, students asked questions about their notes. After answering these questions, Mr. Zack moved back to the podium at the front of the room.

Next, Mr. Zack began to review what students should have in their notes on workers. He asked the students to provide assistance while he put the "bare-bones outline" on the chalkboard again and elaborated on each topic, noting points he had made in his lectures, books he had suggested, and examples he had given.

A student said that she had missed a lecture, and Mr. Zack immediately went to her desk to look at her notes. He confirmed this and suggested that she get the notes from someone else in the room. He returned to the podium and continued this review of his lecture notes.

With six minutes remaining in the class period, Mr. Zack said he wanted "a reaction to this—questions and comments." There was a pause of about five seconds, and then he continued with: "Well, if you don't have any questions and comments, then . . ." [pause] Still, there was no response from the students. Mr. Zack ended the discussion with: "Look over your notes. I want you to be experts on this topic."

This "discussion" session was a class period devoted to recall of what Craig Zack had presented in lecture. The recitation routine assured him that all students, regardless of ability, interest, or classroom behavior, had essentially the same information in their notebooks concerning the main topic.

While social studies teachers said that they gave emphasis to discussing issues with students, lecture and recitation predominated. Basically the teachers covered the same information during both lecture and recitation sessions, with the teacher frequently supplying examples for points made and answering his or her own questions.

Alfred Moore's perception of his work was representative of the other teachers' beliefs about their relationship with students:

> To the extent that I use novel approaches, students take advantage of the situation, because they see the human side of me. Since I can't trade them [i.e., unwanted students] for others, I present myself to them as bland, stern, and businesslike.

These teachers believed that their effectiveness was dependent upon creating a "bland, stern, businesslike" image while teaching. A more personal approach caused students "to take advantage of the situation." Here it becomes clear why teachers who might otherwise be dynamic and creative in their lectures and presentations reduced their work to the level of routine. The conduct of teaching included the use of routines, such as lecture and recitation, as standard means for presenting subject matter to diverse students enrolled in their classes.

Further, the teachers' potential to misuse routines paralleled the students' potential for misbehavior: One form of behavior played off the other. An opposite case in which teachers and students work off each other in a positive way is made by Maeroff (1988):

> The best teaching is predicated on a frank exchange in which the learner openly acknowledges what he or she doesn't know and shares his or her fears with the person doing the teaching. Otherwise the person doing the teaching has no assurance of conveying the information that the learner most needs. (p. 51)

The routines of lecture and recitation at Truman were examples of unselfconscious teacher behavior. It was so much a part of the formal role expectation that teachers tended to use it unreflectively in school. The misbehavior of the high school students was in part a "silly" or "emotional" adolescent response. It was also a result of their boredom or aggravation with teacher behavior. The students' day consisted of making the circuit of classes with at least five different teachers. Having already had ten or more years of experience with schoolteachers, most students had resigned themselves to the rigors of schooling, while a few were recalcitrant. The more serious disruptions and the teachers' preference for routine were telling features in the teacher-student relationship.

Anthony Finley's wife clarified the trouble with such teacher behavior when she described how it translated into "teachy" mannerisms at home.

> When Tony comes home from school, he usually speaks to me in that tone of voice that he uses for his lectures. It's monotone, but authoritative. I roll my eyes sometimes, letting him know I have my opinions, too. And he's too loud. I will say, "I can hear you plainly, my dear. I'm right here." It's happened hundreds of times.
>
> When we have guests over for dinner and Tony starts talking, he will emphasize the main point, like I'm sure he does in class, "The main idea here is . . ." Then, he will go on to list the subdivisions: "We stayed home from the concert last night for three reasons, one . . ." He'll draw conclusions in a conversation, saying, "Therefore . . ." He doesn't do this all of the time, but I find it's real hard to respond to him when he does this.

The teachers become so dependent upon following routines that their habitual way of dealing with students also becomes a part of their personal life. Mrs. Finley's remark about the effect of the routines on her suggests that there was a relationship between the misbehavior of students and the teachers' routinization. Students became frustrated with the impersonal nature of the teachers' presentation and turned to deviant activity to get relief. This vicious circle produced a sense of futility in teachers, and something was needed to counteract these effects.

The work schedule and student subcultures were also responsible for these effects. Teacher and students were together for a whole semester. A teacher could not leave the room during a class period. Conducting class was always a problem because students were often absent, late, or had a reason for leaving early. Sometimes their excuses were legitimate, such as band practice; sometimes they were not, such as drinking alcohol or taking drugs in the parking lot. Since even legitimate absences disrupted an otherwise orderly coverage of content, they were often a source of aggravation for teachers. Student transience created a nightmare for teachers concerned with accuracy and fairness in record keeping and make-up assignments. Also, teachers knew that students would tell their friends about their classes every day, spreading news about anything unusual with amazing rapidity during class-change time. Rumors about teachers had wings in the school.

The teachers' low tolerance for deviant behavior reflected an attempt to protect themselves from failure and embarrassment on the job. If student misbehavior was not squelched immediately, the whole class could become rowdy. If the students got control of a class, there was a high risk of failing to cover the content for the day. And if the teacher did not regain control of the class, the principal would conclude that the teacher was failing to perform duties appropriately, putting the job itself at risk.

Lecture and recitation were examples of the routines teachers relied upon to do their job within the confines of classroom context and school policy, making of these routines standard crafts for success on the job. The teachers justified routine activities on the grounds that the system was inflexible and the students intractable. The more routinized their teaching activities, the more assured they were of getting the job done according to expectations. Also, students thus became accustomed to ordinary classroom protocol, another facet of routine activity. However, the teachers knew that sooner or later someone—a student, a colleague, or an administrator—would disturb the routine. The teachers' adoption of an unsuitable role expectation was a cumulative effect of the system.

Deadness Versus Vitality

The teachers' perception of an external locus of control led to what they called *deadness*. According to Andy Abraham, teachers were suffering from deadness when they "stopped reading and lost enthusiasm; that is, went through the motions and tried, but their heart wasn't in it; didn't teach anything; and didn't try new programs and new ideas." The teachers believed there was a relationship between proximity to retirement and deadness, but they also recognized the potential for deadness at any earlier period in their career. During an interview about the career of teaching, Andy Abraham was referring to deadness when he said to me, "I look at older teachers at times and I don't want to become a Curtis Jasper. That's what time can do to you though. The *routine*. It gets to you after a while."

Deadness was a condition in which a teacher used as common practice what many others would consider unsuitable teaching activities. It was a conscious choice by a teacher to abandon the ideals that teachers had worked out for their formal role expectation. Deadness was an extreme form of reliance on routine that occurred when a teacher, from exhaustion or loss of will, perceived himself or herself to be hemmed in entirely by the situation in the classroom. The social studies teachers feared deadness because it raised doubts about their teaching competence and their subject-matter knowledge. Teachers who wanted to avoid deadness looked to their informal groups for support.

A "dead" teacher was one who gave students questions to answer from their textbook every day but, according to Andy Abraham, "didn't care about what they read and didn't care about reading, period." In the "dead" teacher's classroom there were only a few lectures and discussions during a semester, and these usually pertained to school rules. A "dead" teacher followed the school's curriculum guide minimally, gave multiple-choice exams from the textbook publisher, and rarely gave writing assignments. Andy Abraham summed it up: "They have students read their textbooks and go through the same junk every year." There was an awareness among the social studies teachers that deadness crept into every teacher's work to some extent. But slippage was different from succumbing to deadness. "Dead" teachers were not welcome in either clique.

Within their informal groups these teachers kept alive their concern about teaching and learning. They believed they were a minority group within the high school and felt dragged down by the reputations of dead teachers. Their fear was that they would give up eventually, for the operational criteria for teacher evaluation seemed to define the career exemplar in terms of deadness. Administrators thought of a loud class as a class out of control. Students tended to perceive a change in the routine as a tax on their energy or fun time. The citizens of Rillton wanted teachers to excel in both academic and co-curricular activities. From the teachers' viewpoint, more years of experience meant a greater likelihood that the routine would "get to you."

Vitality was the name teachers gave to the opposite of deadness. It was an ideal teacher role that included a positive attitude and a set of activities to support professional conduct. To be vital one had to study continuously and revise lesson plans in accordance with what the students were to learn. This scholarly endeavor would entail considerable expense of time and energy, for it meant that one should not depend too heavily or too often on a routine. In the opinion of teachers in both cliques, the work schedule at Truman provided too little time for adequate preparation, for fostering teacher vitality.

A vital teacher saw himself or herself as an authority on a subject—a highly valued self-perception. But however desirable vitality was as an ideal, it was costly in practice: To the extent that one focused upon being vital, one's chances of surviving through the school year were in jeopardy. In other words, it was better to focus on a bottom-line concern such as survival. The usual compromise was to maintain partial vitality by periodically updating a subject-matter routine.

Subject-matter approaches took two forms among teachers in the social studies department at Truman High. Teachers in the Academic clique relied upon the "issues" and drew support from various "outside sources" for their work, while the Coaches depended upon a textbook. Each Academic cultivated a special interest, worked it into notes for lecture and recitation sessions, and covered this topic to some extent in all of the different courses and sections. For Anthony Finley it was economic theory; for Art

Heidman, military history; for Arnold Wilkes, nuclear proliferation; and so on.

As the following quote from Anthony Finley illustrates, "breaking the routine" with something from the area of special interest infused the teacher with vitality.

> I read an article like that in *The Nation* and it makes me livid. Goddamn! You know, I was talking to Abraham about it, and I think I *will* teach a nine-week session on the recession. They may get bored with it, but that's too bad. I've usually limited a session to four or five weeks. That's about the limit of their attention. But this is important. It's got to be done. I'll push for it.

For the Academics, current events affected the routine, occasionally altering topics for several weeks. Although to the Academics it seemed like a break from the routine, to the students and Coaches it was old wine in new bottles, since these teachers presented it through the standard lecture and recitation methods. Nonetheless, with the support of others in the clique, a teacher could avoid deadness and survive for nine more weeks.

Among those in the Coach clique, a textbook was the mainstay. The teachers who were striving to be vital developed lectures from the textbook and assigned primary sources to their students as supplemental readings. The routine, at times reinforced with a team-teaching approach, was a continuous marching of students through the chapters of some textbook. While social issues were stressed by the Academics, the Coaches emphasized a chronological survey of historical events.

Because Coaches were involved with co-curricular activities, "breaking from the routine" usually amounted to telling students about recent events—often sports. Yet recounting or discussing such events was frequently more than a time-filler. To these teachers, the congruity of teaching and coaching was so thorough (this was often the topic for a huddle) that it was easy for them to point out to their students the educational implications of some field event, regardless of the subject taught. Deadness resulted, though, when the teacher dwelled too much upon co-curricular activities per se.

Breaks such as these helped the Coaches in the same way that the interplay of specialized interests and current events helped the

Academics. Teachers in both informal groups avoided deadness and gained some sense of vitality by altering the routine in these ways. The activity related to co-curricular activities that was common to many of the teachers reported by Cusick (1983) parallels those of Coaches. Everything came together during classroom instruction for these teachers: the subject-matter specialty, sports, avocations, and so on.

These teachers believed that sustaining a sense of vitality assured them of respect as subject-matter specialists—the teacher's expression of authority in the school. On the one hand, trying to be too vital sapped the teacher. On the other hand, while some routine was necessary for teaching, deadness was the outcome for anyone who chose to disregard the need for revision of subject matter.

The workplace culture of these social studies teachers included an interest in professional growth, but chiefly as this supported stereotypical routines of teaching. There was a thin line that separated the routine from deadness. A distinguishing characteristic of deadness was the teacher's self-conscious choice to use unsuitable activities. Teachers who were in some sense vital would tediously administer an exam. "Dead" teachers would work crossword puzzles after they assigned students to read their textbooks in class. All of the teachers, but most extensively the Academics, devoted time to study during evenings and on weekends in order to preserve a sense of freshness. Both Coaches and Academics depended upon their informal group for the exchange of ideas and for securing support or criticism for plans to stay vital and avoid deadness.

The Trap

In order to make it through the year, teachers had to cope with the fear of slipping into the offensive aspects of some routine. This nexus of attitudes and techniques, called *the trap*, enabled the teacher to achieve some control over subject matter and student behavior—but at the expense of professional conduct. Each clique defined for itself what was offensive about the routines; in this way, clique members could tell when a colleague's activity within a routine indicated that he or she was falling into the trap. The teachers could have used this mutual surveillance to protect themselves from unprofessional conduct and improve the conditions of work. Instead, their collegiality supported competition over ideas about work as well as subscription to a workplace mentality. The four elements comprising the trap I classify as *narrowmindedness, indoctrination, arrogance,* and *roughhousing.*

According to social studies department policy, a teacher was supposed to cover radical, liberal, and conservative interpretations on a given issue. Yet each clique accused the other of presenting a slanted view while reinforcing its own members' biased slant in the opposite direction. The Academics tended to use supplemental readings that presented radical views, but the Coaches perceived this attitude as narrowmindedness, that is, encouraging students to "accept the radical perspective" and "taking a dim view" of those who espoused liberal or conservative views. Coaches preferred to use a standard textbook for all courses, but the Academics saw this attitude as indoctrination, that is, "indoctrinating the students with a conservative political view—patriotic rightwing bullshit." Members of each clique benefited by collectively viewing the other clique as "caught in the trap." This process allowed individual teachers in both cliques to continue giving biased lectures in the name of presenting alternative views to their students.

During department meetings the Academics and Coaches exchanged what Craig Zack called "violent verbalizations" over the question of which side's attitude toward subject matter was insidious. Defending the appropriateness of his methods, Art Heidman said in a department meeting:

> If I were to stand in front of *my* students and say, "This is gospel and what Art Heidman says is so," this does not allow for criticism or examination of the issues. Presentation of alternative views goes *beyond* indoctrination.

The ethos that permitted one clique to use its own classroom bias to "counteract" the other clique's classroom bias contrasts with what Cusick (1983) reports: "Informal associations were never allowed to intrude" upon the contents or methods of instruction used by the teachers (p. 102). The difference in findings might be due to hiring practices. At Truman, teachers fell into two distinct groups with distinct values—Coaches and Academics. Hiring practices by those in Cusick's (1983) research were "a bit casual," leading to homogeneity among the faculty (p. 73).

Art Heidman's statement quoted above notwithstanding, teachers in both cliques at Truman either did not recognize an opposing view when lecturing or, if engaged in an argument with students, were uncompromising. As Craig Zack explained, "When you're a teacher, you can determine what you are going to talk about." Focusing a subject-matter routine was the purview of the teacher. The cliques provided support for continuing approaches to teaching that were just short of narrowmindedness and indoctrination.

Administrators were not without concern. The assistant superintendent said he wanted more "centralization of operations in the school district" and had been coercing the teachers at Truman "to revise, amend, or develop the social studies curriculum for two years." The credibility of the high school social studies department depended to some extent upon the teachers' presenting a united front to the administrators on the issue of curriculum revision. Yet the work arrangements that fostered teacher isolation adversely affected their chances of examining this issue in depth. "Where's the release time for this work?" Clifford Harris asked. The organization of work for teachers, as Lortie (1975) notes, "fosters conservatism of outlook" (p. 232). The tasks that social studies teachers at Truman carried out on a day-to-day basis in their classrooms reflected a conservative approach to education.

Despite the push from superordinates, these social studies teachers believed they could not reach accord. They had an acute awareness of the opposing role expectations among the Academic and the Coach cliques. The one hour per week during which the department met formally to address their work problems was insufficient. Criticism—public and private—led to little creative practice or change in work routines. The informal groups engendered the formal role expectations that guided the teachers' work in the department. Routine activities supported the teachers in their work role and reinforced the status quo.

During department meetings and informal gatherings between classes, teachers in both cliques reiterated their positions and gained support for continued presentation of their preferred views to students. In this way collegiality influenced the social studies curriculum and contributed to the individual teachers' willingness to stay. Art Heidman had this to say about the support he received from colleagues:

> If it weren't for Silvius and Finley, I would have been gone
> so fast it would make your head spin. It's difficult putting up
> with uninformed, ignorant, stupid opinions or attitudes ex-

pressed by so-called intelligent people. We pimp them [Coaches] because they are idiots. They are transmitters of the popular culture, not people teaching students to critically examine or evaluate the actions or institutions of the world.

During a huddle Clifford Harris presented his colleagues with justification for their (political) conservatism:

About six or seven years ago, I was out for a walk at this time of year and passed this house where a Truman High girl lived. She had just graduated from the university. She brought up the subject [radical slant of the Academics] as we stood there in front of her house talking. She was of the same opinion [as we]: how much they were hurting these kids, because they were not being prepared to handle some of the things they were being told.

These teachers felt confident about support from other members in their cliques regarding their classroom activity. When they were teaching class, both Academics and Coaches felt secure about giving biased views to their students. The students recognized and expected biased lectures from their teachers. As one student explained:

It happens in the social studies department as a whole. They are very closed, narrowminded people, who do not recognize it themselves. They are more set in their ways and unwilling to admit it. Openness is what they always preach, but it is the opposite model that they present.

Yet if one of the students adopted such an attitude in class, as sometimes occurred, classmates were quick to respond. The result for one teacher when such mimicking took place was that the class—an elective—began to disappear. As the teacher explained the event: "Last semester two students became arrogant bigots in class. They made all of the others feel like dumb shits. The word got around about this and now I hardly have anybody in here." What the students were rejecting was behavior by classmates which mirrored that of a teacher who had fallen into the trap.

The social studies teachers also depended upon their cliques for development and support of techniques for controlling student activity in classrooms and hallways. Each clique viewed with disdain the other clique's method of control. Teachers in the Academic clique used what Coaches called "arrogance." The Academics accused Coaches of "roughhousing" students to control behavior problems.

Arrogance accounted for Anthony Abraham's position as leader in the Academic clique, a technique that led to the mannerism that in Chapter 3 I called "distancing." Art Heidman explained his use of the technique as follows: "I'll test people and within one or two questions I'll know if they are a peabrain and if they are, I won't say any more." Others in the Academic clique behaved similarly when interacting with students and Coaches. On a number of occasions I observed their tendency to put some kind of distance between themselves and another person in order to end a discussion or dispute. When done in class with students, the teacher was able to maintain tighter control of a topic's focus. When done during interactions with Coaches, it squelched any possibility of dialogue.

The following example indicates how a teacher used the technique of arrogance with students:

> During class a student asked the teacher if he believed in ESP. "No," was the teacher's response, cutting off the student. The teacher continued his lecture. After class two students who believed in ESP met the teacher at the door and brought up the topic again. The teacher refused to discuss the question and, after the students left, remarked: "Every class is like that. I always talk to the wall in here. They are thoroughly beyond reason. Sometimes they get rowdy, because I refuse to give up time for that stuff. It's such a damn *waste* of time."

This was the teacher's rationale for distancing himself from the students' topic. These teachers wanted to cover the topic prepared for a lesson and to maintain the preferred focus—their view of a radical perspective. Once class was over, they could dismiss a "peabrain" idea from students with a further display of arrogance.

The Academics displayed "arrogance" toward Coaches as well. In one situation, Carl Stevens, who was discussing conservation of natural resources, noticed arrogant mannerisms in the behavior of Alfred Moore—looking away, delayed or no response to a question, and increasing physical distance between them. Mr. Stevens soon departed. Afterwards I asked Alfred Moore if he had wanted to hear the whole argument from Carl Stevens.

"Well, not really," he said.
"Then you weren't listening to him?" I inquired.
"No," said Alfred Moore.
"Do you have a low tolerance for other people during a discussion?" I asked.
"Yeah," he answered. "That's all he [Carl Stevens] knows. If you ask questions of him he won't know what the hell you are talking about. Ask Silvius if you don't believe me. They [Coaches] are all dumb as posts."

To students and Coaches the display of arrogance by Academics signaled the end of mutual involvement. It allowed Academics to retain control of a topic's focus in lectures with students and to shorten the duration of their interaction with Coaches.

Both uses of arrogance contributed to the style of work by Academics. Yet, according to Andy Abraham, one had to guard against "jumping on students for petty things; that was the trap for teachers." Teachers in both cliques showed a low tolerance for deviant behavior among their students. The Coaches defined what was offensive about routines used by the Academics to control their subject matter and student behavior. A display of arrogance (often including a terse remark) from a teacher in the Academic clique was sufficient to deter a miscreant.

The Academics found equally offensive the technique used by Coaches to keep student activity within limits—*roughhousing*. Students who misbehaved could expect to receive punishment through seating rearrangement, removal from class, or even corporal punishment. The use of roughhousing was a frequent topic for Coaches when huddling. The teacher who told of its application could gain assurance from colleagues that the action was justified. Those who listened benefited by increasing their repertoire of variations on the roughhousing technique.

The following is illustrative of how and why a Coach might rearrange students during class:

Clayton Samuels spotted two girls who were talking to one another. "Are you two girls friends?" he asked. One girl said that they were. "Then you switch with her," Samuels said while pointing to a girl in the next row and one seat forward of her position. The students exchanged places. "There," Samuels continued. "Now you won't get yourselves in trouble in here."

For a more serious infraction of the rules (persistent talking in spite of rearrangement, for example), the teacher would send the student out of the room with a desk, to wait in the hallway until class was over. If, as in the following incident, the student became obstinate, the teacher used corporal punishment or the threat of it.

> During lunch Clayton Samuels came in and said to Carl Stevens: "I heard you roughhoused a kid."
> "It wasn't much," Carl Stevens replied. "The kid would not sit in his assigned seat and claimed he didn't know where he was supposed to sit. I tried to get him to move and he wouldn't, so a push-shove conflict developed and I was the winner."

The slapping incident that I reported in Chapter 2 was an extension of the above. That is, the push-shove conflict could turn easily into slapping, wrestling, or even a bout of fisticuffs. The activity reported here is similar to that reported by Cusick (1983) about a teacher in his study who used a "hard physical line toward students" (p. 81). Coaches used the roughhousing routine to keep student activity in line with rules established for classroom conduct. If students behaved, then the teacher could proceed with the lecture unimpeded. Roughhousing was a back-up technique that helped teachers maintain control over deviant student behavior.

Because Coaches were known to use roughhousing to control what they took to be inappropriate student conduct, Academics felt uneasy around them. As Art Heidman explained:

> You can't trust them—I don't come close to them; they're too emotional. I was in the lounge one day and got into an argument with Carl Stevens about something and I thought sure he was going to hit me. His face got red, he was shouting, and coming at me. I had to leave.

Consequently, Academics were cautious about getting into arguments with Coaches. Those in the Academic clique used pimping as a subtle way of annoying Coaches. But, as the following incident indicates, when someone from the Academic clique pimped a Coach, the Academic was quick to back off.

"What can you do to get me an increase in pay," said Art Heidman, a member of the Academic clique.
"Get rid of department heads," said Clifford Harris, a Coach.
"How about getting rid of athletics?" Art Heidman said, pimping Harris.
"All right. I didn't hit your area," Clifford Harris said, increasing the volume of his voice.
"I didn't mean it to be taken personally," Art Heidman said.

Coaches were athletic. They kept in good physical shape through weight lifting, running, swimming, and so on. One could appreciate why those in the Academic clique were cautious when pimping Coaches. The object of pimping was to gain a little satisfaction, but not at the expense of personal injury.

Summary

Both cliques had developed attitudes and techniques for achieving some control over subject matter and student activity in classrooms. Lecture and recitation were predominant methods of instruction. Coaches interpreted an emphasis upon so-called radical views by those in the Academic clique as narrowmindedness. Academics interpreted the perceived conservative slant offered to students by Coaches as indoctrination. Arrogance and roughhousing were techniques that the teachers developed principally to achieve some control over student activity, although they also adopted them for use with members of the opposite clique.

The apparent discrepancy between the teachers' beliefs about their work (different content and methods) and their reflective perception of work (lecture and recitation) begs the question: Why did they interpret their actions in a contradictory manner? Teachers in both cliques expressed concern about educating youth, but they viewed themselves as caught in a dilemma. They had entered the field of teaching to provide high school students with instruction in social studies. However, the characteristics of students, organization of the workday, and policies of the institution tended to divert emphasis from the pursuit of academic interests and place it on management of students. The teachers, especially those in the Coach clique, cooperated in this endeavor, but they resented the extent to which custodial responsibility dominated their work.

The teachers used standard techniques in managing the behavior of students and biased attitudes in covering subject matter. To the extent that the teachers misused these techniques of control, they exacerbated the students' tendency to misbehave, thus reinforcing their dependence on routine and leading to offensive or unprofessional practice. Perhaps, if the institution had held the teachers and students more accountable for making important decisions, then custodial responsibility would have been only a residual concern (cf. Kanter, 1977). Perhaps, if the teachers had better understood their relationship to the institution, if they had perceived themselves as lacking an understanding and skill with higher-level decision making, then they might have been more resistant to choosing unsuitable or inappropriate practices and more inclined to reeducate themselves (cf. Schrank, 1978). Instead, control of the school's work organization remained in the upper reaches of its hierarchy. This structure denied responsibility for decision making to teachers, who passed their disenfranchisement on to students, creating a self-perpetuating cycle of disrespect. In this way the institution showed a disregard for the role of reflective thinking in the practice of teaching and the ability of teachers to do reflective thinking. Teachers found some relief for their frustrations through the conscious use of unsuitable teaching behavior.

These teachers fully intended to offer the best instruction they were capable of every day. Yet the nature of teaching in the high school sapped them of energy, making avoidance of deadness a mainstay for survival. Even the most respected members of the cliques were on the verge of deadness and fearful of falling into the trap before the end of the school year. Success on the job was reduced to survival. The routinization of teaching activities gave the illusion of accomplishing a formal role expectation in accordance with the ideal. In reality it stood for a desperate dependence upon teacher mannerisms and supported a myth of professional conduct. These work circumstances led some teachers to take drastic measures to obtain relief.

CHAPTER 5

Escape

One Thursday evening in April Alan Silvius invited me to join him and four other teachers for a meeting with the school board at which they were presenting a teacher's grievance on non-renewal. I accepted. The meeting started promptly at 7:00 P.M., with Mr. Silvius presenting his arguments first. Fifteen minutes later the school board and superintendent told the teachers to leave the room because they wanted to go into executive session to make their decision. Five minutes later the recording secretary told the teachers they could reenter the meeting room to hear the result—denial of the grievance.

On the way out we met an assistant superintendent who had arrived too late for the first order of business but knew about the matter. "We won," Alan Silvius said, playfully pimping the administrator. "I know better than that," the assistant superintendent said. He informed me the next day that it was a standard procedure for the administration to consider in advance all issues for discussion with the school board and, whenever possible, to agree among themselves beforehand on their position and the reasonable and legal arguments for support. Alan Silvius knew this and had done his best to prepare counterarguments, but he lost. He had lost many times.

"We usually go out and have a couple of beers after one of these," Alan Silvius said to me as we were leaving the building. "You want to join us?" he asked. I said yes. He took me to a place that was a favorite spot for teachers, the Lamplighter Inn. At the bar he ordered the first round and told me that he could have only two beers because he had to drive back to Idolville and get up at 5:00 A.M. for another day of teaching. We talked in a general way about the cases he had pursued for teachers. He believed that in most instances their grievances were reasonable, the exceptions

85

being those concerning teachers whose work he knew was poor or unprofessional. "We need to do something about that. It does not help our image," he said. Then Alan Silvius shook his head, took a deep breath, and continued.

> I'm tired. I've been working on this case in my spare time for the past two weeks, evenings and weekends. You saw what happened tonight. We lost. We usually lose because of a legal or technical matter. The board has a lawyer on retainer. We are on our own most of the time. I know next to nothing about law.
>
> But that's not the half of it. I've fallen at least four weeks behind on my preparation for teaching. Today I collected over 100 term papers from my three American history classes. Tomorrow I give exams in the two political science classes. That means I will have more than fifty written exams to correct. Do you have any idea how long it is going to take me to read all that stuff? My wife and kids are asking me if I am still a part of the family.

He paused while looking into the mirror behind the bar. The other teachers who were part of the grievance proceeding, who had been sitting at a table, were leaving now. They waved and said good night to us as they went out the door.

Alan Silvius had something he wanted to tell me, but guardedly. He lowered his voice and continued.

> I've got to get back in touch with my wife and kids this weekend. I'll do the exams and papers during the evenings, but it's going to take a couple of weeks, with all of the reading that I need to do for preparation. And there is one other thing. I have got to take a "mental health day."

I asked him what he meant by that. He explained that there was no provision for teachers to get away from the urgent matters of schooling during the day in order to collect their thoughts or to resolve a crisis. The time between classes was too brief for recovery. The bell would ring, the students would enter the room, and the next lesson had to go on. The teachers' lounge offered a poor opportunity for renewing one's strength. The contract gave some protection from intrusions during the lunch period, but one could always expect an interruption from an administrator, student, or parent. He added: "Who can say 'No' when some little problem they bring will snowball and ruin your whole day?" An experienced teacher could feel the trap closing. A mental health day was a safety valve that protected teachers from the worst effects of the system, but it was not in the contract.

"What are you going to do?" I asked. "Why don't you come along and you'll find out?" he said gamely. I stopped to think about his proposal and ordered our second round. "Okay," I said. "What will we do?" He gave me the instructions quietly.

> I go to the outdoors at a time like this. The trout season is open and I love to fish. I know a great place, even if the fish are not biting.
>
> It's also the flu season. Next week you are not going to feel well. Thursday you call in sick at 6:00 in the morning. Bring your gear and I'll meet you in the parking lot of the Idolville mall at 6:30. Make sure your lesson plans are caught up and on your desk. And don't tell anyone.

We had plans for a mental health day. Alan Silvius seemed to have gained an improved outlook already. I was curious and a little concerned about my job. It was time for us to leave. As we were getting into our cars he said to me, "There's one more thing. Don't forget your fishing license." His warnings were more important than his instructions.

The next week I saw Alan Silvius briefly on Wednesday, when we were passing each other in the hallway among the throng of students. He winked at me and I winked back. The mental health day was set. Thursday morning I called in sick and headed for Idolville. There was a heavy fog, which helped to conceal my departure but made me late. Alan was waiting for me in his father's old station wagon. He had the back window open, so I tossed in my gear. "Got a thermos of coffee up here," Alan said. He was driving away before I could slam my door shut.

It took an hour to get to the stream. The fog remained heavy, and the route took us from a state highway, to a county road, to a dirt lane, to a forest path and into the next county. Alan parked the wagon under a dead-end sign that was nailed to a tree and immediately got out to put on his waders. I could hear the water moving nearby. It sounded like a slow, deep stream. "The sun will burn off this fog in the next hour or so," Alan said while strapping on his creel and dip net. "The stream is right there. You go down.

I'll go upstream. We'll meet here at noon." Before I could say anything, he had disappeared into the mist.

It took me nearly an hour to get ready. I had borrowed the equipment, because I seldom went fishing. The lines, lures, rods, and net were all in a tangle from the rough ride, and I had not rigged anything earlier. Finally, all was ready. I put on the waders and walked into the woods. Near the stream there was a winding path that was muddy from the regular visits of others who had come here to fish. I followed this path and turned onto one of its side paths going toward the stream. Dense underbrush was everywhere, making it almost necessary to crawl over the bank.

I stepped out to the water's edge and surveyed the area. The stream was only twelve or fifteen feet wide. Downstream there was a sandbar and immediately upstream there was a sharp turn where the water had gouged a hole in the bank under an ancient sycamore. A deep pool would be under that tree root, a very good spot for trout. But how would I get there? I would cross the stream and walk up on the opposite bank. This decision almost proved disastrous. The spring rains had made the stream full and its banks were nearly vertical from erosion. I put one foot in and touched bottom in a frenzy when the water reached my crotch, lost balance for an instant, and regained footing with both feet precariously lodged on the roots and mud of the bank. Cold water had splashed into my face and soaked my clothes. A slender birch branch was hanging overhead, so I grabbed it to steady myself and take a second survey of the area.

It was Thursday at 8:45 A.M. If the substitute teacher was following my plans, the students in freshman English were getting a lesson on the parts of speech. I was up to my elbows in this stream, three feet from the bank, and barely holding on with a twig against a forceful current. It was funny and it was not so funny. I had dropped the fishing tackle on the first slip, and the stream swept it away. How could I float if my waders were full of water? I wondered how many teachers had drowned while fishing on school days and what the newspapers reported.

The roots and mud were disappearing fast from under my boots. The tiny branch was strong, so I pulled myself gradually up the bank, until I was able to climb out. Then, I sat on the muddy bank, dangled my feet in the water, and laughed out loud with relief. "If only my students could see me now," I thought, "in this crazy, exciting predicament." Strangely, the fact that they would never know gave me a good feeling. That one step into the stream

was a risky but intensely personal experience. It helped me understand the value of a mental health day. The work life of the high
school teachers was so much a part of their students' lives that it
was difficult for the teachers to separate themselves from the
adolescents.

For the remainder of the morning I walked along the stream
and searched for wildlife. The sunshine and warm air brought out
a profusion of birds, frogs, and salamanders. A moth fluttered
above the water and disappeared in a fish's splash. I regretted the
loss of the gear, but I didn't miss it. At noon I returned to the car.
Alan had just arrived and was putting his gear in the station
wagon. "Catch anything?" he asked. I told him about falling into
the stream and we laughed. He told me that he didn't come here to
catch fish, but to play with them. There were no hooks on his
equipment. He derived satisfaction from luring the fish to him.
Once in a while he would get lucky and succeed in netting the fish,
but he always threw it back into the stream. "It's a fair game: no
hook, no hurt," he said. "The object is to outsmart them, although
they almost always win." We got in the car and drove to a diner for
lunch.

Alan Silvius took a mental health day to get away, to escape
from the classroom routine. He believed that there was a benefit
for his students as well as for himself. "It saves them from me and
saves me from myself," he said. The standard practice of teaching
created a tense atmosphere in the classroom that eventually would
impair the interaction between teacher and students. The daily
class meetings took place in accordance with a regular schedule.
The assignments, examinations, and grades built up high levels of
anxiety and false or unrealistic expectations among students and
teachers. The childish antics of the students were as constant as
they were magnetic. It was common for an ordinary sequence of
events to bring the teacher and the students into something Alan
Silvius called a "combat situation." He elaborated as follows:
"When school is in session, I am working day and night and many
weekends to stay on top of things. There are times when my
students and I are at each other's throats and it is best that we
separate and cool off for a while."

The system was the source of this problem, but the system
offered the teachers little relief. The administrators, counselors,
and specialists had some control over scheduling appointments
with students. They could determine when a meeting was to start
and when it was to end. Also, they could shut themselves up in

their offices when they needed to prepare a case or to recuperate privately. Flexibility and alternative scheduling were not a part of the teachers' workday. At the sound of the bell, teachers were to commence instruction. A preparation period and a thirty-minute lunch break were the only exceptions, but they were immovable fixtures in the schedule. Illness was one of the few legitimate, personally controlled reasons for teachers to postpone work with students. If they could break away from the classroom routine for a long enough time, they could preserve or restore the professional aspect of their work. One way to escape was to feign illness.

In *Small Town Teacher* (1972) Gertrude McPherson used the category of "evasion" to explain how elementary teachers occasionally deviated from existing rules. In all instances, the teacher sought privacy, and the two conditions necessary for engaging in evasive or defiant activities were "informal group support and a social situation incompatible with existing rules" (p. 178). The mental health day that Alan Silvius showed me was similar to McPherson's finding. I use the expression *escape* to indicate that there were differences from what McPherson reported. Even though there were risks associated with the defiant act, to Alan Silvius and his colleagues the reward was worth the risk. Also, their escapes from the classroom routine were regular and frequent, not occasional, occurrences. Although the teachers usually did not take mental health days together, individual teachers could rely upon their informal group for identification of opportunities within the two types of escapes: *built-in* and *secret*.

An expression that Alan Silvius and his colleagues used to justify their escapes was the need to "feel fresh" for their work in the high school. From the teachers' perspective, it was important for them to feel fresh for the job, but school authorities did not recognize this need and the work schedule did not provide adequate relief. The need to feel fresh led to the search for ways to take advantage of built-in and secret escapes. In general, these measures were unsuitable and inadequate.

Feeling Fresh

When the buzzer announced that it was time for him to start another class, Andy Abraham looked up at the speaker and said, "You can't escape from that damn thing." Whatever the topic was for a lesson, the teachers had considerable pride in doing work in the name of educating youth. They felt constantly responsible for managing a classroom full of students for five periods, each forty-seven minutes, every school day. However, as Andy Abraham explained, "You're responsible for the mood of the class, and there is a tremendous drain to psych yourself up for a performance when you are not fresh." This work with adolescents drained the teacher. Late in the day or on days when one felt badly, the drain was worse. The teachers believed they needed to avoid this.

The drain affected Coaches as well as Academics. Craig Zack addressed the problem of feeling fresh from his clique's perspective:

> One of the biggest stresses in teaching is the day-by-day being pumped up, being enthusiastic, and, of course, the stressful one where, twice this year already, someone might be insubordinate or you get a rebuff from the administration when you think you have an answer to a problem and it is not accepted by them. Those things can really eat away at you long after you leave the "trenches."

The role of teaching required constant interaction with an adolescent audience whose responses were often forced or unwelcome. Within this tenuous relationship, teachers also had to grapple with repeated presentation of subject-matter content. The result was exhaustion and stress. Aspects of the teachers' work that the administration controlled (for example, class assignments and the daily schedule) were sources of emotional and psychological drain.

When the buzzer announced the beginning of the first class period of the day, it set into operation a series of sharply punctuated, odd intervals of time toward the end of which every teacher worked. Even if one felt fresh at the start of the first class, some measure of freshness had drained away by its end. By the time the last class period of the day got under way, the teacher was beat.

In the same way that the first buzzer marked progression toward the end of a school day, the first work day in August marked progression toward the end of the school year. The teachers did not always attribute the drain of freshness to interaction with students in the classroom. As Andy Abraham explained, this also happened because the "administrators keep loading more and more crap on you." With two months of work remaining in the school year, teachers said "it's survival" in answer to how things were going. With one month of work remaining, there was little interest in students, colleagues, or anything having to do with school.

Getting to the end of a class period, a school day, and a school year demanded conservation of freshness. To satisfy this need these teachers searched for ways to escape from the classroom routine. It was an informal role expectation that the teachers valued highly because the best coping strategies helped teachers to forestall the drainage. At the end of one class, Craig Zack described his lecture to me as follows: "I don't know if you noticed last hour, but I was not doing what I had planned. I was too tired. This hour was the same. You need to be fresh to do a good job." When freshness was receding, it was important to get away from the situation through a strategy of built-in or secret escape.

Built-in Escapes

One kind of escape was built right into the lesson plan. As the following example demonstrates, it may appear to be a way of capturing the interest of students.

> Each day at the start of class Arnold Wilkes read a poem from an anthology. He had not yet made the selection for this day, and so he picked one. As he looked over a poem, he said to me: "The class has gotten to the point of really liking these readings."
>
> As he read the poem, one girl was reading from a paperback, another was working on her bibliography cards, and other students were busy with similar occupations. A few appeared to be listening while sitting up, slouching, or resting their heads on their desks. At the end of the reading Mr. Wilkes said, "That was a bit obscure." There was no discussion.

Variations on the above built-in escape pattern allowed the social studies teachers to forestall lecture or recitation routines until they felt ready to begin. While some built-in escapes had a remote linkage with the subject matter planned for the course, others had none. For example, on the first day of classes after the spring break Art Heidman cut his lecture short and gave his students handouts that would be used for the current lesson. Mr. Heidman distributed the handouts one page at a time and passed around a stapler for fastening the pages together. While this was going on the students were free to engage in conversation among themselves. Mr. Heidman clearly had no intention of continuing the lecture or engaging in any discussion. The time devoted to this exercise with the handouts exceeded twenty-five minutes. Teachers in both cliques repeated variations of this escape pattern during the semester. It allowed them to take a break while working in the trenches.

Whenever the administration planned an assembly, the teachers could count on a built-in escape. At the designated hour all teachers and students were in their respective classes—everyone was waiting. Because of the organizational effort the administration thought was necessary to move so many students to one location, teachers knew that there would always be time available for a break before the bell announcing the assembly; likewise, there would be time after they returned to classes. Typically, teachers used these leftover periods (ten to fifteen minutes) for no object lesson. They used this time to preserve freshness.

Teachers resented being required to serve as monitors for study hall sessions and transformed the assignment into an escape. As Clifford Harris explained after settling the students down, "Now I'll doze off . . . R and R [rest and recuperation] period." He spent the entire period alternately nodding, watching for misbehavior, and dozing.

Department meetings were another ordeal from which to escape. All one needed was an appropriate excuse and an unwillingness to endure the meeting. One excuse was co-curricular activity; another was a student. For example, when a student came up to Alan Silvius after the last class of the day to talk about his lecture, he told Alfred Moore to pass on word that he would be there "late or not at all because of the student."

At mid-year the administration planned a two-day in-service session for the professional development of all teachers in the district. Teachers deftly changed this event into an escape from the classroom routines. During the first day's morning coffee break Craig Zack, with his colleagues nodding assent, explained the experience of escape at an inservice:

> This is where I have to be. I don't mean that derogatorily.
> It's just a statement of fact. It's a nice break from the
> trenches, especially this time of the year [winter]. The ad-
> ministrators don't trust teachers to do academic type things

and they're right. Nothing else gets accomplished at these sessions.

In-service sessions, assemblies, department meetings, and faculty meetings punctuated the continuous involvement between teachers and students. The school authorities determined the timing, order, and content of these meetings and required the teachers' attendance. The teachers, though, considered time thus spent to be wasted. Time was valuable to these teachers. If they were not involved with instruction, then they needed time to prepare for it. Thus they often turned what they considered wasteful time into productive time. For example, they would correct papers and exams during faculty meetings.

The social studies teachers used built-in escapes to remain vital for work in school. The nature of these strategies suggested that there was at least a remote link with professional activity. They were relatively easy to identify and administrators, aware of the tendency for teachers to take advantage of escape mechanisms, looked upon the practice disapprovingly; but they rarely took corrective action. When an administrator uncovered a secret escape, though, it was a different matter. These activities infringed upon formal rules for teacher conduct in the school, and some form of punishment followed. Truman's teachers were wary of being discovered in a secret escape—and for good reason. The seriousness of the teachers' need for relief became evident in their choice to break rules at the risk of losing their jobs.

Secret Escapes

Secret escapes were clandestine activities that the teachers believed were their last resorts for preserving freshness and were critical for their survival. The school authorities did not approve of them; a teacher's discovery in a secret escape could lead to dismissal. Regardless of the consequences, members of both cliques frequently took part in them. As with other aspects of their formal and informal role expectations, the teachers often could count on the cliques to identify, facilitate, and offer protection for an escape. While there is reason to maintain a sympathetic view of these escapes, this coping strategy was nonetheless an example of unprofessional conduct.

The shortest and simplest secret escape was for one teacher to step into another teacher's room during class time to talk about something that was thought important, whether of a humorous or serious nature, yet was unrelated to work. Both teachers might be holding class at this time. Taking a mental health day was an example of a complex secret escape. Teachers used this large block of time to acquire solitude and get away from school and teaching. They went fishing or shopping far away from Rillton or worked on hobbies in their homes. As Alan Silvius indicated in regard to the fishing trip, the teachers had to be careful in their execution.

The principals and central office administrators were aware that teachers executed secret escapes and dealt swiftly and severely with anyone they discovered. For example, Clayton Samuels decided to play sick during the in-service session and use the two days to repair his antique rocking chair. On the second day he needed some glue and drove at 1:30 P.M. to the local hardware store for a new bottle. It was a fatal oversight. An assistant superintendent happened to be having a late lunch at the front window of the plaza's cafe. He spotted Mr. Samuels driving his red Buick and stepping into the store. The next day this administrator gave Mr. Samuels a stern rebuke, informed him that he had jeopardized his job, and placed him on intensive supervision for the remainder of the year.

In another instance, a secret escape raised legal and ethical concerns because it involved embezzlement. Alvin Schumacher had approval and support to attend a conference in another part of the state for two days. After registration he decided against attending, returned to Rillton, and stayed at home. When he submitted the form requesting payment for conference fees and travel expenses, the principal asked him for details about the event. Mr. Schumacher eventually confessed that he had returned home because he "was not feeling well." His failure to call in sick led to an inquiry, conducted personally by the superintendent, that uncovered the real circumstances of the teacher's return: "a coincidental illness, convenient for skipping work and receiving unearned pay." The result was a harsh penalty: loss of all benefits associated with 123 accumulated sick leave days and a dock in pay for the conference period. In the opinion of the superintendent, this penalty was "lenient." He told me that he wanted to dismiss Mr. Schumacher from his job immediately to set a precedent, but he chose not to pursue that route because he was too involved with related litigations.

The principal expected teachers to be in school throughout the time specified by the bargaining contract. However, there was no time card to punch and, with eighteen entrances and exits to the high school, one could slip in late or slip out early without detection. Teachers could legitimately leave early by signing out in the principal's office, but they resented the watchdog role assumed by the principal and preferred not to have the record of legitimate built-in escapes become too long. They had developed a way of avoiding this red tape. Members of the Academic and Coach cliques would secretly escape after the last class of the day through exits in the shop, art area, or field house.

Those who rode in car pools found it particularly difficult to work out a strategy whereby four or five teachers could simultaneously escape unnoticed. But they did so. Art Heidman explained the procedure as follows. Arrangements had to be made days in advance, the car had to be parked in a certain location in the morning, and when walking from the building to the car one had to affect a gait (a quick one) suggesting that one's intentions were "good." Despite difficulty, the teachers were often successful. As the event described below illustrates, though, they could be caught in a collective effort to leave early from school. Although the teachers expected that there would be consequences, these results were unknown and the teachers regarded them fearfully.

> During third period Alan Silvius was called out of class by Art Heidman, a member of his car pool. "Art, you look like you are going to be sick," Alan said. Art explained that when they were leaving early from school the previous day, Vincent Holmes had checked the sign-out sheet and found only one teacher's name on it—Alan's. He had "Vinced" Art about this matter in the lounge, and Art's only defense was that he was under the assumption that Alan had signed all of them out. Art's message was that the assistant principal expected to see Alan before he left for home.
>
> Alan explained to me that the clique had an understanding that whenever one of them needed to be home for some kind of appointment, he signs himself out, never signs all of them out, and takes full responsibility for the consequences, should there be any. No one complained. If the event was planned a day or so in advance and somebody preferred to stay in school, he drove himself in for the day. They had not been caught before.

On the way to his meeting with Vincent Holmes, Alan expressed his opinion to me as follows:

"I'm furious. This is one of those nitpicking things that administrators do to teachers. I'll admit that it was against the contract, but we are trying to save on fuel and wear and tear on our cars. It's complicated to organize everyone. There are teachers who don't give a damn about teaching and bartend until 2:00 A.M. and sleep in school. When I am at home, I put work into preparing for my classes. I strive to be vital."

Throughout the meeting with Vincent Holmes, Alan was apologetic and conciliatory. Near the end Mr. Holmes said, "It is school policy that people sign out and *you* [the clique] should do it. If concessions are made for any individual or group, the whole faculty will want the same privilege. This is *not* to be repeated."

"I agree," said Alan. After the meeting Alan had two words of exclamation: "That prick!"

Teachers knew that they were risking their jobs in a secret escape, but they believed the advantages outweighed the disadvantages. They worked with others in their cliques to develop ways of avoiding discovery. When caught they felt angry, for secret escapes were important breaks in the routine of school—they helped teachers conserve freshness. Accused of such a wrongdoing, a teacher protected members of the clique by taking full responsibility for the infraction, exposing neither the plan nor the rationale.

The administrators knew that teachers engaged in secret escapes, considered these activities to be examples of unprofessional conduct, and took immediate punitive action against those who were found out—usually a verbal reprimand, but occasionally intensive supervision or nonrenewal. The administration did not exercise its right to dismiss a teacher during my research, but the superintendent had considered this option seriously on at least one occasion.

The teaching contract gave teachers the right to be absent from work for an illness or school-related business. As soon as possible after learning of a teacher's impending absence, the administration would hire a substitute teacher. On the face of it, one would think that this institutional mechanism would solve the problem regarding freshness. There was even a clause in the contract accepting emotional disturbance as a legitimate illness.

In the opinion of the teachers, the right to be absent for illness and
the hiring of a substitute were good faith efforts by the authorities,
but they fell short of meeting the teachers' needs and were less
than effective for the students' instruction. Andy Abraham spoke
as follows about the problem:

> We don't take days off unless we have to and then we plan
> ahead for a film or a quiz or just reading the textbook. Some
> of us keep a special set of plans just for subs. Let's face it,
> how can a substitute teacher take over my classes when it's
> usually somebody who's never seen these kids before and
> may know next to nothing about the subjects I teach? There
> are some subs who can maintain control of the room, but it's
> usually at the expense of content. How can they help it?
>
> A teacher absolutely hates to get sick. Of course, nobody
> wants to be sick, but when a teacher has to miss work sud-
> denly, it can screw up the schedule and destroy a class. Have
> you observed a substitute teacher's class lately? It's bedlam.
> Last week when Arnold Wilkes was out for a strep infection,
> I had to go down to his room three times to help the sub get
> the class under control. For a while it sounded like they were
> going to kill him. I mean that literally.
>
> When the first class walks in and sees a sub, they know
> what to do. The word that you have a sub spreads like wild-
> fire among the kids. They look upon it as a day off, a free-
> for-all. When you return to work, the kids let you know that
> "nothing happened." The bottom line is this: You get sick,
> they have the day off, and you dread seeing what's waiting
> for you when you return. It's a farce. There has to be a better
> way. If the public knew one-twentieth of what passes for edu-
> cation they would burn the place up.

In the opinion of teachers like Andy Abraham, the provision for
substitute teachers was a misdirected, stopgap policy. Teachers
needed relief for days when they were ill or when they were away
for professional meetings, but the scheme built up false expectations. The substitute teacher could not take the place of the regular classroom teacher, except in instances of long-term replace-
ment. However, illness and professional meetings were not the
main concerns of these teachers; freshness was. In their opinion,
the day-to-day operation of the system produced a form of institutional illness that interfered with the teachers' effectiveness. One

needed to escape from the classroom routine in order to preserve or restore the freshness necessary for the practice of teaching.

Summary

These teachers could expect cooperation from their colleagues when the need arose to escape from the classroom. Some escape mechanisms were built into plans for the school curriculum, and to take advantage of them was an easy step for the teachers, with few or no unwelcome consequences. Other escapes were secretive, and the teachers took serious risks when choosing to conduct themselves in this manner. Both patterns of escape were examples of unsuitable or unprofessional conduct. That these activities had evolved within the cliques and that they continued to be a part of this teacher culture indicate the importance teachers attributed to feeling fresh for their work with students. These coping strategies, which derived from the teachers' fatigue, both arose from and contributed to a workplace mentality.

What kind of a guiding idea is operating when the workplace culture sanctions a clandestine search for ways to avoid teaching in order to sustain oneself in the professional capacity? It is a contradictory, self-defeating idea about the teacher's role. Truman's social studies teachers were aware of the seriousness of their contract to teach youth. They also knew how risky were their efforts to stay vital. The teachers might not have been so inclined to escape if the circumstances of work had been different, more respectful of human needs. They might have chosen more positive ways to put some distance between themselves and the irksome or monotonous aspects of their work. The authorities approved of decision making, flexibility, and alternative scheduling for their own administrative role in school, but denied these and other privileges to teachers (see Darling-Hammond, 1988). The school secretaries had better access than teachers to information and processes that would affect in important ways the teachers' world.

The definition of professional conduct that the administration used for teachers was simplistic and was in contradiction with the operational demands of the school system (see Herbst, 1989). Teachers were to conduct themselves in a professional manner in all aspects of their work, but they were not permitted to make decisions about matters that were important to their work, notably, scheduling classes with students, limiting the duration of instructional periods, and gauging the time they needed for class preparation and the time off they needed to stay fresh. Ostensibly, the administration's control of these decisions provided assurance that the school would operate in a smooth and regular manner. However, the teachers' informal conduct suggests that this policy of executive privilege was an instrument for upholding the authority of the school board and administrators, enabling these officials to maintain without compunction an inequitable, undemocratic institution.

For the superordinates, teaching involved running Truman High School at its lowest level of operation, according to the same rules that were established for the adolescents—follow instructions, maximize time on task, work according to a rigid schedule, and so on. These are a schoolmarm's conditions for work. To punish all for the possible mistakes of a few is a commonly known teacher mannerism. The administrators—former teachers—converted this caricature into a principle for the operation of their school. Administrators treated teachers as well as students like wayward children. Deprived of the professional privilege to think reflectively in support of their classroom activity, the teachers used it regularly in support of deviant behavior and thus got relief from the system.

CHAPTER 6

Benign Neglect

On a Friday evening I met Craig Zack at the Truman gymnasium. He had invited me to a girls' basketball game between Rillton and its chief rival, Idolville. We took seats in a remote section of the bleachers so that we could watch the game and also talk about the high school teacher's work. Many of the parents and students who crowded into the seats closest to the hoops recognized Mr. Zack and waved to him or shouted, "Hi, Coach!" Craig Zack was known for his commitment to co-curricular activities. He had been coaching boys' baseball and girls' tennis since he started teaching nineteen years previously.

A loud, dull buzz from the timekeeper's horn called the two teams out on the floor for the tip-off. After the referee put the basketball up, Rillton's center flipped the ball to her guard, who raced away for a lay-up, scoring the first two points of the game. The bleachers trembled with the crowd's response. There was a low level of continuous cheering and a deafening roar the instant one of the players made a basket. Cora Chapin, the girls' basketball coach for Truman, was pacing the gym floor and shouting excitedly to her team. This would be a close game. At time-outs and breaks, Cora Chapin would rush into the center of her team, giving the girls instructions and exhorting them to fight hard and fair for Truman.

Craig Zack talked about teaching throughout the game, interrupting himself during decisive plays and intense cheering from the crowd. He began by gesturing with his outstretched arm to the whole gymnasium, now nearly full of people.

This exposure outside of the classroom after hours is good, if for nothing else, to build relationships that you wouldn't get if you confined yourself to the classroom. You get acquainted with the community at athletic events like this one. The payoff here for Cora Chapin is recognition and acceptance. Community interest revolves around athletics and that puts the coach in the limelight.

However, there are about as many bad things as there are good things about this setup. On the good side, there are very few coaches who can't walk down the street and be known and spoken to by large numbers of townspeople. That's very different from the experience of the classroom teacher, whose only involvement with people is with those kids in the classroom. On the bad side, most of these same people would not realize that the coach also teaches every day. They don't think about how this investment in coaching affects the teaching of social studies. They think that all this person does is coach.

It is really difficult to become known as a great teacher. A number of very good schoolteachers influenced my life, but if I go back to my hometown and talk about these people, nobody will know who I'm talking about. I might be the only one who sees their effect. That's a very different career from the basketball coach who took our team to state for the championship. That's someone who everybody in town thinks of as great and remembers.

I have a lot of respect for the Academics because they are good at teaching social studies. They work hard staying up-to-date on their specialties, just like we work hard at coaching. The sad thing for all of us is that we can't be excellent in both teaching and coaching.

The result for our department has been so much bickering and protecting of territory. Some of us have made our classrooms into sacred shrines. The rest of us have caved in to the community's interest in highly visible programs, like athletics. The school board and administration give the public what it wants. One day it's mainstreaming students. Another day it's accountability for teachers. Who knows what it will be next? These are serious problems for our profession.

We spend so much energy trying to protect our little domains. We're turf-fighting against ourselves. I think we're taking care of the kids who are good athletes and strong scholars, but what about the vast majority who are not in those two categories? A great many students are falling through the cracks, while we fight over petty concerns.

Too many kids become nothing more than numbers for the school system. Some kids end up in serious trouble. They prove to us that everybody loses in the long run. You should look up Billy Radman. He was a good kid, until he got into trouble. He was a student in one of my classes, and I feel bad that I couldn't have done more for him. I think he's still in prison.

You may perceive teachers to be very outgoing, but they are not. They won't say boo about something that really matters in their work. This has always puzzled me. I used to think that teachers were very strong individuals and would be strong forces in their community. You have to be strong in the classroom, but it doesn't carry over into the public arena. Why is it that we teachers can't do that?

Everyone was standing during the final three minutes of the game. The score was tied, then Rillton was ahead by two points, then Idolville took the lead, and then it was tied again. This contest would be won in the last five seconds. Idolville's center put the ball up too high on the board. Rillton's forward stole the rebound and whipped it down court to her guard, who sent the ball swishing into the basket just as the horn blasted, ending the game. The roar from the crowd was like a jet engine at take-off. Cora Chapin's home team had beaten Idolville, 58–56.

We congratulated the coach and her team for the fine game they played. I thanked Craig Zack for sharing his thoughts about teaching. The tendencies toward bickering and protecting territory that he raised as an issue would be typical of workers in any occupation. However, a fixation on petty concerns in the face of the personal and institutional problems he referred to would indicate that the teachers' activity was inconsistent with role expectations for professional conduct. Mr. Zack believed that he and the other teachers were good at what they did but were capable of doing much better work. He also believed that there were aspects of their work that made teachers inept at dealing with adults, particularly in relation to improving education.

Billy Radman's story revealed the potential consequences of this benign neglect for students and the Rillton community. It also helped explain Craig Zack's concern for his colleagues and the profession of teaching. The police had arrested Billy Radman on the school grounds the previous year and charged him with possession of illegal drugs with intent to sell. In common parlance, he was a drug pusher. He was also a member of the senior class at Truman. The police began surveillance of Billy's activities after finding his phone number in the apartment of a stripper who had died from a drug overdose. Billy's trial led to a conviction on narcotics trafficking, and the judge sentenced him to serve one to three years at the Tri-County Correctional Facility.

When I met Billy in the visitors' room of the prison, he was willing to talk about his past involvement with drugs. The police record, including a confession that helped to reduce his sentence, corroborated the story he told me. Billy's involvement with drugs stemmed from a dysfunctional family life. His parents and older siblings used drugs and had arrest records. He began selling drugs at Truman during his sophomore year and quickly expanded his operation to most of the Rillton community. He had a variety of customers, some of whom were other high school students.

As a senior he spent most of his days at the high school. He would cut classes but remain in the building or on the school parking lot for sales. He sold any drug that the customers requested and his supplier could make available to him, including liquor, LSD, and marijuana. His contact had a reputation for making rapid deliveries and using cruel tactics. "I sold everything possible to anyone," he said. Billy had been told that if he ever had trouble collecting a sum of money from a customer and it was a substantial amount, all he had to do was let the contact know and he would send in a man who was an expert at removing identifying characteristics from people. "This man was a butcher," I said. "Yeah, I guess that's a pretty good name for him," he added. Billy's dealers were from out of state and had connections with organized crime.

Billy Radman remembered his teachers from Truman, including Mr. Zack. When expressing his opinion about high school, he said that he could only speak for himself but he believed that his friends held a similar view. He said:

> If you weren't into the sports scene or wild about going to
> college, it was a drag. My friends were there and that was
> great. We found our own things to do. I got busted one day
> for selling a lousy joint. I'd get back into it, but the stakes
> are too high on the mob side. The law is a deterrent. This jail
> sucks. I can't wait to get out of here. But it ain't nothing like

the mob, man. There's a good chance I'll get paroled in six weeks.

Most students at Truman were not like Billy Radman, but to Craig Zack and the other teachers, he was a symbol of their failure to deal responsibly with a majority of their students. The institution did not permit a teacher to have a positive effect on many students—very few, in fact, compared with the number of students for whom a teacher had responsibility during the year. The social studies teachers identified themselves with either the academic or co-curricular program. Due to the competitive nature of both programs, only a small number of students could receive close supervision from their teachers. A majority of students identified with neither of these concerns and relied on their peer-group activities for satisfaction. From time to time their abandonment led to dangerous conditions for individual students, Truman High, and the Rillton community.

Billy Radman's perception of the students' life at Truman complemented that of his teachers. Even though Craig Zack and the other Coaches had a commitment to the low-level students (as discussed in Chapter 4), they perceived themselves as having too little effect on the whole student population. Teachers in the Academic clique expressed a similar view about their effectiveness. They would say that a teacher was lucky to have a student in class who demonstrated clearly that he or she learned what the teacher had to offer. About his work, Andy Abraham said: "My failure rate is about 99 percent. Well, maybe that is a little exaggerated; 95 percent is closer to the truth. You can't succeed in this job. You can only fail." The teachers' disappointment stemmed from a variety of sources, including uncertainty about the outcome of their work, a feature that is endemic to teaching (see Lortie, 1975), and a workplace mentality in the place of a professional culture.

The system was also partly responsible for these results. The design for instruction suggested that the teachers could have a positive effect on a large number of students. The high school's policy statements and curriculum materials emphasized "centralization of opportunity, equality of opportunity, and individualized learning," giving the impression that every student would receive the highest personal challenge. The teachers' work schedule involved teaching five different sets of thirty to thirty-five independently assigned students in forty-seven minute intervals for a total of 150 to 160 students per day. The class schedule and the school language fostered the image of Truman High School as a smoothly running physical plant for the controlled, equal, and high quality batch processing of students. In reality, it was a small percentage of students who derived high levels of personal satisfaction through the academic or athletic programs and a large percentage who became the custodial responsibility of teachers by default of the system (see Darling-Hammond, 1988).

The teachers' frustration with the manner in which the institution set them up for disappointment and failure led to feelings of cynicism and self-doubt. Despite the specific nature of the teachers' contract to provide social studies instruction, the area of their responsibility for professional service was large in reference to any individual student—Billy Radman was an exception—and immense in reference to the revolving groups and varieties of students. The teachers perceived their professional responsibility to be vast—that is, multifaceted instead of specialized—and increasing. Their response was to place a high value on superficial domains and to protect these from encroachments by students, other teachers, and the school authorities.

The teachers' pettiness, pursued with little reexamination or relief, distracted their attention from their responsibility to define the teacher's role in terms of professionalism. The benign neglect that was characteristic of the teachers' treatment of the students paralleled the treatment the teachers received from the institution. Their behavior in reference to four territories—subject matter, classroom, gym, and professional library—exhibited the costs to themselves and the lost opportunities for Truman High.

Subject Matter

These teachers thought of themselves as social studies specialists. Regardless of how good or poor their university preparation, they were proud of this image and their protection of other territories could be seen as extensions of their activities with their subject-matter specialty. Carving out and defending a niche in social studies was a typical and natural aspect of a teacher's work, because a secure specialty gave the individual an identity at Truman High and some protection against shifting or nonrenewal. However, the department's defensive behavior entailed conduct that was inconsistent with the teachers' professional interests. It was typical for the cliques to quarrel over control of the social studies curriculum, for individuals to distribute material in a discriminatory manner, and for all the teachers to use excessive measures at times to control class time.

The usual reason for holding a social studies department meeting was to answer two questions: What should be taught? Whose subject matter is it? When the teachers addressed these questions, Academics and Coaches would pit the radical perspective against the conservative perspective for control of social studies territory. Teachers in both cliques conceded that they had been fighting the same battles for many years. Craig Zack described his department's meeting history to me. He said,

> Our department meetings must have been the closest thing to war in the whole central part of the state. They were volatile and verbal. We had many meetings when people would pound on the floor and walk out. Nothing was accomplished. There was a very big clash—there still is.

During these clashes the Academics said that they were trying to change the focus of the social studies curriculum so that it would cover all political perspectives, but the Coaches accused them of "trying to ram something through" (in service of their radical perspective). The Coaches said that they were resisting the proposals for change, because the status quo represented a healthy balance, and the Academics charged them with "stonewalling" (in defense of their conservative view). Both cliques were striving to impose their views exclusively on social studies content. Ordinarily the department meeting is a professional activity, but for these teachers it was an arena for unscrupulous pursuit of narrow and self-serving interests.

For instance, a stonewalling tactic on the part of Coaches would bring an abrupt end to a proposal for curriculum change from the Academics. To illustrate, about thirty minutes into one meeting, Clayton Samuels loudly and angrily interrupted Art Heidman's presentation:

> "All right. Your mind's pretty much made up. Is that what you're saying?"
>
> "No. We are looking for the thrust of the junior high and senior high schools and seeing how this thing all fits together," Art Heidman answered.

"I disagree wholeheartedly! You're trying to ram something through in a week, period! I think it's ridiculous. This
is much too serious a problem to get it through in a short
time by slapping down some idea on a piece of paper," Clayton Samuels shouted.

"We have already done a lot of research. We are beyond
that. We've been on this for three years," Art Heidman said.

"But you're wrong! You've been bringing this in here and
it's not what we worked on. If you're asking us to come up
with a whole redesign in a few days, then say it's your own
committee's. That's the way your committee has been operating anyway. Don't pawn it off as our work. To ram it
through in one week is ridiculous," Clayton Samuels said.

Stonewalling by teachers like Clayton Samuels involved arguing
for more time, complaining that the committee had involved only
a few people from the Coach clique, and charging that the contents
of the proposal were false representations of input from supporting sources, such as administrators and elementary or junior high
school teachers. Never mind that they, the Coaches, had not volunteered to be on the committee to reform the K–12 curriculum. The
cumulative effect of these arguments was postponement of the
point at which a decision would be made. Meanwhile, Coaches
were confident that the Academics would not be able to take their
social studies territory away from them.

Aspects of the ramming technique are also evident in the above
example. Clayton Samuels and the other Coaches did not believe
the Academics' three years of work on the proposal to be innocent
of bias against them. Academics showed impatience with the process for change in the department and, working within their
informal group, devised ways to rush things through. Not only did
others believe the Academics operated clandestinely; they themselves admitted to the practice in private conversation. The following incident involving Arnold Wilkes shows how Academics attempted to trap obstinate and unsuspecting Coaches.

During one department meeting Arnold Wilkes said that a
committee he was representing needed some information about
courses from everyone in the department. He got up from his seat
and distributed a questionnaire to all members. While passing out
the sheets he said loudly twice: "Be sure to put your name on it, so
we can come back to you for clarification." When the meeting was
over and all the teachers had gone home, Arnold Wilkes told me:

We're just waiting for the questionnaires to be returned, so that we can read what these other people [Coaches] put down. Just wait. What they put down they are going to be held to doing. I can't wait. They are not going to put something up to us that we haven't seen ten times before. We want to know *who wrote what* on those papers. We've run it.

As his use of the pronoun *we* indicates, this was an organized effort by the Academics. Effectively carried out, this looting scheme would secure all highly valued subject matter territory (namely, senior-level college-prep courses) for sustained members of the Academic clique. Art Heidman offered further explanation:

The bottom line with this proposal is that Coach courses will be reduced to electives. They [Coaches] will do anything to prevent that. If that happens, then kids won't take their courses and they will have to teach required American history courses for sophomores and juniors. That means maybe I'd take over teaching all seniors and have a few juniors.

The Academic clique was using this strategy to take highly valued social studies territory from Coaches. The benefits to Academics would be greater job security, satisfaction, and prestige. Coaches used stonewalling for the same effect.

The teachers' territorial behavior was evident also in their exchange of content-area readings, films, guest lecturers, and so on. The sharing of instructional material always occurred within cliques. While addressing this concern one day, Andy Abraham explained that he and the other teachers in the Academic clique considered the photocopying machine to be "an absolutely indispensable tool," making it possible to "get away from the textbook and have academic freedom." In a matter of minutes after finding an article in some magazine or newspaper, they could have a copy made for every student in class. "In that way," Andy continued, "we don't have to summarize these things and then lecture on them—students read it themselves and it is so much better."

However, he and his colleagues were selective when distributing this material to other teachers, for the material itself was an important part of their territory. For instance, while Art Heidman was using the photocopying machine, he spoke as follows about copies he made of a recently published article on Central America: "I don't give this out to every rum dum in the building.

There are only 10 percent who are educable. I only give it to people I think there is any hope for." Those 10 percent were members of the Academic clique. Instructional materials were an important part of a clique's subject-matter territory, and the teachers guarded them carefully.

Teachers also felt called upon to defend their subject-matter domain in classes themselves. Although the time allotted to class periods was determined by the administration, students, colleagues, and administrators themselves would interfere with the time set aside for instruction. When called on at a strategic moment, a student might announce, "Linda's gonna be sick" or "Jason said he's bored stiff." A serious quarrel might erupt suddenly between two students or between the teacher and a student. The equipment necessary for a presentation might fail. A colleague might appear in the doorway and do a monkeyshine. In regard to the latter, the teachers would tolerate members of the same clique. They did not steal time across clique lines. The phone might ring, since the school secretary was notorious for calling teachers at any time during a class period to inquire about absentee records, missing students, and rescheduled appointments. At seemingly random moments the principal would blare announcements loudly over the PA system. No matter how strong the desire for uninterrupted teaching, there was always a good chance that something would interfere with the teachers' lesson plans.

The teachers resented these interferences and had worked out ways to prevent the theft of instructional time. They protected the time for class preparation as well as the class period itself. On the one hand, this represented an expected and ordinary response from the teachers. After all, it was their job to teach social studies and they needed time to cover the material. On the other hand, in some instances the strategies and the manner in which teachers used them were poor adaptations to circumstances.

When the bell rang announcing the start of class, teachers wanted to give uninterrupted attention to their lesson. Even though they might be having an involved discussion with a colleague during class-change time, they would terminate the conversation abruptly. For instance, one day during the three-minute transfer period Carl Stevens was expressing to Cora Chapin his frustration over inadequate preparation time. When the last student entered her room, Cora Chapin interrupted him in mid-sentence with, "My attention is divided now. The students are here." She immediately shut the door to her classroom and began taking attendance.

It was common for students to interrupt the teacher at any time during a lesson to request that the class do something other than what the teacher had planned. In the following example Clifford Harris explained how he argued with his students one day about what to do during class time—what they wanted or what he had planned. He related this view of the event:

> At the same time that the fourth-hour sociology class was scheduled to meet, all students in the school were invited to attend a presentation given by one of the men who had been held hostage by the Iranians. The class begged me to take them and they got rowdy, because I refused to give up the hour for that.
>
> I said no, because it was not what we were studying and I saw no educational value in it. They said, "We are not going to do what you want us to do." They got downright obnoxious and I lost my temper a little bit. I said, "I'm used to talking to the wall in here anyway, so if you want to turn your desks around and face the wall, you can and I will continue to lecture anyway." All but four did and I conducted my lesson as I would have had they not turned around, and it went that way for the whole hour. They were quiet.
>
> When the bell rang, they turned their desks around without my telling them to and went out without saying much at all. Just kind of walked out with frowns on their faces. I said, "Thanks for being such a good class. Every class should be like that." It was better that way, actually. At least I didn't have to look at them groveling in self-pity.

Sometimes teachers met an intrusion on their time with willful resistance. Usually, when students made a request at the start of class to discuss a current, but only remotely relevant, topic, the teacher would say, "That is the last thing I want you to do. What I want you to do now is take out your notebooks." Whether against encroachments from administrators, teachers, or students, these teachers believed that it was their duty to safeguard the time for instruction. In principle, these measures gave some assurance to the teachers that students would receive social studies instruction. In practice, strategies like these neglected educational benefits that stem from honest and open inquiry with students; they were, however, instrumental in protecting the teachers' little domains.

The Classroom

As one would expect, the teachers' place during the school day was the classroom. The administration had assigned each teacher a particular room within which to give the students instruction. There were no offices for teachers. However, for these teachers being in the classroom was more of personal choice than an administrative assignment. Indeed, their use of the classrooms signified a peculiar sense of ownership. The classroom was a physical territory for presenting specialized knowledge and a sanctuary for obtaining relief from the institution. The lack of responsibility for decision making may explain the high school teachers' use of institutional furnishings and their generalized activity in reference to classrooms. It is typical of workers in other occupations to rearrange furnishings and add things to their workplace, such as photographs and knickknacks, that express personal preferences and exhibit a flair for artistry. These are ordinary acts of territorial behavior. The wholesome effects of this expressiveness include pride in one's work and a sense of belonging. In some respects the activity of these teachers was like other workers. The social studies teachers referred to their classrooms as personal domains. For example, while rearranging the desks in his room one day, Andy Abraham asserted, "This classroom is my turf." There were also some differences.

The teachers determined the contents and position of the equipment for each classroom, including the teacher's desk, student desks, bulletin board displays, maps, cabinets, and bookshelves. However, the possibility for variety was low because the rooms and furnishings were standard sets, the schedule of classes was rapid paced and inflexible, and a gridiron setup would facilitate the flow of students to and from classes. As a result, the teachers' classrooms showed much in common. Student desks were in five or six rows facing the teacher's desk, chalkboard, and podium. Bulletin board displays—rarely changed during the year—included school rules, emergency information, VIP photographs, posters, and magazine or newspaper clippings. Also, personal artifacts, such as photographs of spouses and children, were not in evidence. Almost every item in these classrooms was a piece of school property that had a direct and obvious relationship to social studies. One might ask why the teacher, much less the students, would dwell in such places for personal satisfaction.

The administrators had prepared a schedule of classes that was effective and convenient for them in the organization of the school day, the enrollment of students, and the assignment of workloads to teachers. To a social studies teacher, the schedule was like a deed to a classroom, with lessons serving as the currency for mortgage payments. Andy Abraham taught in Room 259, located in the west corner on the second floor of Truman. Figure 6.1 illustrates his daily schedule.

When I first entered Room 259, Andy Abraham said, "This is my classroom." Although it was like most others, there were subtle reminders that a teacher was at work. Within these walls he conducted classes, met with parents, confided in colleagues, and prepared lessons. If it was not time to teach, Andy Abraham was in his classroom alone and, though his door was open, his demeanor expressed a preference not to be disturbed by anyone. Before period one and after period seven, he sat at his desk correcting student exams and term papers, writing, or reading some book, magazine, or newspaper. He preferred not to be disturbed because he never had sufficient time to prepare for his teaching. Occasionally a student would ask for help or one of the teachers in the Academic clique would stop in to visit. In the main, he did not mind these intrusions.

The administration turned Art Heidman's classroom into a study hall during his prep period and scheduled Clayton Samuels

FIGURE 6.1. *Schedule of Classes*

Teacher: Andy Abraham	*Home Base*: Room 259

Period 1:	History
Period 2:	Sociology
Period 3:	259 (Homeroom)
Period 4:	Sociology
Period 5A:	Lunch
Period 5B:	Preparation
Period 6:	Economics
Period 7:	History
Period 8:	Conference (parents, students, or department)

as proctor. When Mr. Heidman received notice of this assignment, he said, "The administration put Samuels in here as a subtle form of punishment for me. This is an intolerable intrusion." From the teachers' viewpoint, the administration was aware that a class-room belonged to a particular teacher. To cope with his disap-pointment, Art Heidman always left his room before Clayton Samuels arrived and returned only after Mr. Samuels had left. So long as Mr. Heidman was absent from his classroom, he would not perceive Mr. Samuels to be infringing on his domain.

In general, pettiness characterized the cliques' use of all spaces in the school. For example, teachers would pass members of the opposite clique in the hallways and occasionally express greetings, but they would not enter one another's rooms, unless it was for a study hall assignment or a department meeting. Also, the infor-mal groups had some influence on a teacher's assignment to a classroom and its use by different members of the social studies department. One response of the principal to the department's infighting was to assign Andy Abraham and Craig Zack to rooms on opposite corners of Truman's second floor.

There was a reciprocal relationship between the teachers' ten-dency to focus on superficial domains or petty concerns and the rules governing their work at school. In other words, ridiculous teacher conduct complemented ridiculous rules for work. The administration had established the rules for teacher movement during the school day and their use of classrooms, but the teachers did not always obey these rules. For instance, the only time that teachers could leave school legitimately was during the thirty-minute lunch break. If they chose to leave, school policy dictated that they sign themselves out in the principal's office, tell where they were going, and sign themselves back in immediately upon returning. Records indicated that teachers seldom left school dur-ing the day, and on those few occasions when they did leave, it was on some business for the school. The teachers' response to the administration's fetish for monitoring their movements was to leave school without recording departure time or destination—to effect a secret escape (see Chapter 5).

It was against the rules for teachers to eat lunch in their classrooms, but many teachers ate lunch there secretly, either alone or with a colleague. When doing so, the teacher would close the classroom door, turn out the lights, and sit at the back of the room in a student's desk out of sight. This stratagem protected the teacher from discovery, should anyone look through the narrow window next to the classroom door. Carl Stevens had this to say about eating in his room:

> This is *my* time in *my* territory. Back here I can belch out loud if I want to. I don't have to excuse myself. I can stuff food down and not worry about what someone else thinks about it. It gives me a chance to be in a situation where I don't have to deal with people for a while.

To Mr. Stevens and his colleagues, the classroom was also a sanctuary. The schedule of classes that hustled students in and out of their rooms, the demands for preparation, and the accumulation of assignments all contributed to an urgent need for relief. For approximately thirty minutes per day some teachers would make their classrooms into exclusive preserves for backstage life (cf. Goffman, 1959).

Truman's policy concerning school management was an important source of the teachers' tendency to break school rules. The administration operated the school according to a set of standard rules that they had designed primarily for controlling unruly adolescents. They expected teachers to abide by the same set of rules, in order not to offend students with a double standard. However, the administrators had adopted a different set of rules for governing their own conduct. This other set of rules gave administrators autonomy for scheduling and visiting with parents, faculty, and staff anywhere in the Rillton school district. Also, the administration used executive privilege to control or change aspects of the school program that, strictly speaking, were the teachers' responsibility. For instance, the administration put pressure on teachers to pass students whose record of achievement showed they were failing. When a teacher refused to comply, the administration changed the students' grades. The formal organization of the school and the deportment of administrators supported the impression that administrators were superior to teachers and were not their peers.

Another example of questionable school policy affected the practice of teaching itself. While the administration and the school board reserved the right to bar the public, including teachers, from attendance at certain of their meetings, nearly every aspect of the teachers' work day was open to public scrutiny. Indeed, the administration periodically used newspaper articles and radio talk shows to remind the Rillton community of a standing invitation to visit Truman High School and "witness their education dollars at work." The teachers had to accept that any visitor who had the principal's approval could observe their work at any time. These social studies teachers worked with a mild level of fear— tempered by experience—of surprise visits from peevish administrators, irate parents, and state department of education officials.

The availability and use of phones and rest-room facilities exhibited most starkly the contrasts in amenities for administrators and teachers. Every administrator's desk included a telephone that allowed the caller to make long-distance and local calls. The communication system available to teachers consisted of an intercom in their classrooms and one telephone for the whole faculty in the teachers' lounge. Concerning this telephone, the administration had given teachers instructions to use it only for brief, local calls. For a long-distance professional call, teachers had to obtain permission from an administrator, make the call during their free time, and use a phone in the principal's office. Otherwise, teachers were to use the pay phone available to students and visitors at Truman's entrance.

Concerning rest rooms, there were men's and women's facilities on the first floor reserved for the administrative staff. The principal's office had a private bathroom, complete with a shower. · On each of the first and second floors of Truman there was one men's and one women's single-stall rest room reserved for faculty. The teachers' hurried use of these rest rooms between classes was one of the only aspects of their day that entailed privacy. However, as Arnold Wilkes pointed out, most teachers had a desperate need to use the rest rooms between classes. Teachers frequently found it necessary to use the students' rest rooms, which offered no privacy to the user. Otherwise they would wait to use a private rest room until the lunch break or the end of the workday. Institutional arrangements such as these undermined the teachers' professionalism and discounted their status as adults.

Gym and Professional Library

One way in which the social studies teachers dealt with their status as unacknowledged adults was to make private use of school facilities. During the lunch period Coaches converted the gym into an exclusive area for exercising. According to Clayton Samuels, their use of the gymnasium "was necessary to get some form of exercise, to stay alert, and get rid of aggression." Craig Zack said, "This is one way to preserve freshness. I'm more relaxed and less reactionary, particularly when I'm with the students." Twice weekly he and Clayton Samuels skipped lunch to lift weights together. While these teachers secretly monopolized the gym, teachers in the Academic clique made the professional library into a private study for the same purpose—to help them restore freshness and maintain better self-control when dealing with students. Through these strategies the teachers made up for the absence of ordinary personal and professional amenities in their work life.

The teachers' use of these areas during the school day (especially the lunch period) often involved a secret escape because it redefined the rules stipulated by the teachers' union and the school authorities. The teachers contract stated that, "Teachers may leave school grounds during the lunch period [forty-seven minutes in total], but shall devote lunch period time in excess of the thirty-minute period to professional responsibilities." To administrators the term *professional responsibilities* signified a wide variety of clerical and custodial tasks, such as record keeping or hallway supervision. To the Coaches it meant an opportunity once or twice each week to spend part or all of their lunch period running, lifting weights, using gymnastic apparatus, and so on. To the Academics it meant retiring to the professional library to read a newspaper or journal, mull over a lesson, or nap.

The following record of a trip to the swimming pool by two Coaches conveys a sense of the need and urgency associated with this activity.

Calvin Miller and Carl Stevens had made plans to use the Truman pool for a private swim during lunch. I had been invited along by Calvin Miller, who was leading me hurriedly through the hallways in search of his partner. "This is not strictly legal, but it helps to get some exercise," he said. "I must find Stevens or I can't go swimming this week," he continued. We looked in the locker rooms and coaches' offices. Finally, we found Carl Stevens shooting a basketball in the gym. "Where have you been?" Mr. Miller asked. "We have to hurry, if we want to get in today." They had missed one another by a few minutes when independently searching the locker room.

They ran into the coaches' locker room, changed into swim suits, and ran to the pool. I sat in a chair with their towels. As he prepared to dive, Calvin Miller told me to keep time and watch for administrators. They swam five laps and their total time in the water was seven minutes. "It was worth it," Calvin said as he pulled himself out of the pool and ran back to the locker room. While they were dressing, Craig Zack and Clayton Samuels entered. They had been lifting weights. Yet another Coach, Clifford Harris, stepped out of the shower.

"See, there's one of the fellas that run," Mr. Miller said, pointing to Clifford Harris.

"This is what's called mental health," Mr. Harris said. "We got until ten after twelve. That's when the last bell rings."

"I'm swimming with Carl on Mondays and Wednesdays now," Calvin Miller related to Clifford Harris.

"That's easier than running," Mr. Harris said. "I don't have enough time to cool down after a run. A quick shower isn't the answer."

"I have to do this. I have the blahs," Mr. Miller said. The first buzzer sounded. "This is it! Now we've got three minutes," Mr. Miller said while tying his shoe. He left the coaches' locker room and headed for the hair dryer mounted on a wall in the students' locker room. He slammed the button with his hand and shoved his head into the stream of hot air. Mr. Harris, left behind, yelled: "Well, you could at least wait for me."

"What time does it say up there?" Mr. Miller asked me.

I looked up at the clock on the wall and said, "12:07."

"What time is it *exactly*?" he shouted back.

"12:07," I yelled, so everyone could hear.

"This is cutting it pretty close. That clock's slow," Mr. Miller said.

"It's every man for himself," Craig Zack shouted.

Mr. Miller's hair was still wet when we left the gym. He combed it while we took the most direct route to his classroom. At the bottom of the stair to the second floor he had less than one minute before the second buzzer sounded announcing the start of his class. He raced up the stairs and was gone.

These teachers made the gym into a private zone during lunch and regarded their exercise routine as a secret escape that was necessary for restoring freshness. The brief and clandestine exercise in the gymnasium gave the teachers something that was lacking in the organization of their workday—the opportunity to associate informally as adults.

Collusion of clique members was a typical aspect of most escapes, but the teachers' takeover of the gym shows it to be a crucial matter and emphasizes the lengths to which teachers went to make up for the system's benign neglect. A key to understanding the teachers' recreational activity during work hours was the rule from school authorities regarding use of the pool, namely, no one was to swim alone. To avoid potential injury and loss of the opportunity due to discovery of a contract violation, Coaches did not exercise alone in any way. They also avoided contact sports or high-visibility sports, such as basketball, because of the noise and potential for injury. Since a secret escape of this kind meant leaving the classrooms, the teachers who went to get exercise needed a decoy and an alibi in the event that a principal would come looking for them while they were absent. To avoid discovery, a teacher who was not exercising would decoy the principal on behalf of the others. When pressed about a teacher who was absent, the decoy would give the principal the agreed upon alibi (e.g., in the john, running off material, making a phone call, and so on). When the teachers returned to their classrooms, the decoy would tip-off the teacher with a message like, "You were Vinced at noon."

The door to the professional library was behind the stacks at the far end of the IMC. Because of its remote location, it was unlikely that administrators, colleagues, or students would go there to find teachers. On the tables and shelves of this small room were popular and professional newspapers, magazines, and journals. There was a large table with chairs, end tables, and four stuffed chairs. A phone and a wall clock appeared to be conspicuous. Except for an occasional visit by a member of the IMC staff, the Academics were the only faculty whom I observed using this small room. These teachers expressed a distinct preference for using the room for private study. When they entered for a brief visit, they did not want to be disturbed by anyone. The professional library was a place where these teachers spoke to one another rarely, if at all, and only out of courtesy. When I was searching for Andy Abraham one day, I found him in the professional library reading a book. I asked if he had time to talk and he said, "I see you found my hiding place." He agreed to the interview, but not in that room.

When Academics were not teaching, they preferred to devote their time to reading professional journals, current events magazines, newspapers, and books. However, the administration would set aside no time in the day for teachers to *study* their subject matter. Teachers had the equivalent of one class period (forty-seven minutes) per day to prepare for instruction and another period to confer with students and parents, hold department meetings, pull hallway duty, and run errands. These periods were inadequate, even for their intended purposes. In actuality, they were hectic periods, during which a teacher would race through the hallways to a variety of locations to pull hallway duty, make phone calls, collect resources, review records, copy articles, and hold conferences. These teachers did not have secretarial services available to help keep records, schedule appointments, and prepare materials.

In the opinion of Alan Silvius, the authorities for the school "took a dim view of the teacher's preparation period," that is, they did not trust teachers to study. The schedule was a false and misleading representation of a teacher's role, and the contract emphasized the teacher's responsibility for custodial work, production and distribution of materials, and record keeping. Periodically, these teachers hid in the professional library because they felt overwhelmed by demands that were unrelated and detrimental to their practice of teaching. The teachers' use of the gym and professional library was an expression of their need to recoup from an institutional effect I call *benign neglect*. They used these and the other domains to preserve a sense of dignity while working at Truman High, ironically passing on their contribution to benign, institutional neglect to the students.

Summary

The social studies teachers at Truman High behaved in petty or defensive ways in reference to particular areas and aspects of their work. Each clique had worked out strategies for keeping what it had and laid plans for taking valued "possessions" away from the other informal group, the most highly valued territory being required senior-level courses. With the backing of their respective clique, teachers bickered for exclusive rights to it. They also made their classrooms into domains for displaying their expertise and the gym and professional library into secret areas to obtain relief or to associate with other adults. They might have used this stolen time to encourage self-reflection on their different but complementary forms of classroom practice, thereby giving themselves and their students different sources of support and reasons for taking pride in Truman High School.

Teachers like Andy Abraham and Craig Zack saw the contradiction between an ideal role expectation and their practice. The responsibility that these teachers had toward the students and the community was enormous, but the school's organizational structure and policies denied teachers their status as professionals and treated them like the adolescents. The activity of the teachers was an expression of their inadequacy to address and resolve some serious problems facing teachers. Teaching social studies meant fighting against other teachers for exclusive rights to superficial domains, contending with frequent disruptions, and coping with contradictory role expectations. To some extent the teachers themselves were culpable. Their response to existing conditions emphasized unprofessional activity. They worked with a fear of discovery in unsuitable conduct and blame for inadequate teaching. However, the institution was also responsible for these results.

Truman's organizational structure and policies were subtle mechanisms that cast teachers in the role of unauthentic adults, bringing loss of self-esteem in its wake and causing even the more responsible teachers to transgress the bargaining contract. The schedule and the authorities controlled the teachers' use of facilities for both professional and personal activities. The teachers' workday involved nearly as little discretionary power as the students' and for the same reason—so that the administration could manage the school for maximum efficiency and minimum disruption. The school's management policies supported a caste system, with separate rules for administrators, presumptuously manifesting their superiority over teachers. The teachers' territorial behavior had less to do with developing a sense of pride or belonging in support of professional conduct than it had to do with finding relief from unfair institutional practices. A hidden dimension of the unselfconscious teacher mannerism was its function as a coping mechanism for the teachers' eventual inability to solve some longstanding organizational problems and appropriately address the most serious occupational hazards of teaching.

People create ways of dealing with whatever circumstances they face while at work and elsewhere. This cultural process leads to the definition of formal and informal role expectations that are specific to a situation and useful to everyone involved. When a school puts teachers near the bottom in terms of authority, it implicitly encourages them to search for ways to cope with a condition that, by definition, is unfavorable to high-quality teaching. In spite of the teachers' intention to do good work in such circumstances, their informal system may support a subculture that enables them to survive but may be in conflict with educational aims. A true and equitable partnership between schoolteachers, administrators, and the school board could have a profound impact on negative institutional effects impinging on everyone's work life at school, especially teachers and students.

CHAPTER 7

Between Today and Tomorrow

This portrait of the social studies department at Truman High has revealed aspects of a teacher's work life that are both real and irritating. The teachers derived benefits from the district through their employment and contributed to the formal educational program by holding classes, attending faculty meetings, and supervising hallways. Work, however, entails more than the completion of designated tasks. At the informal level the teachers relied upon small groups for a sense of belonging and for acquiring perceptions and coping strategies that gave them some assurance of continued success while at work. Some of the latter were supportive of educational aims, while others, prankish and inappropriate, led to an overall image of the teachers that was contradictory, if not foolish.

The teachers at Truman High were aware that their conduct expressed a resistance to craft pride and professionalism. They were faced with a frustrating dilemma: wanting to be professional, and yet conducting themselves in unprofessional ways to cope with the workplace. Like teachers everywhere, they were getting knocked down on three fronts by the institution: occupying a subordinate position in the organization, enduring the low esteem attached to the supervisory role with children, and working in isolation from other adults. These teachers knocked themselves down on a fourth front by conducting themselves in unprofessional ways. How could they expect to be taken seriously when they engaged regularly in activities that tended to detract from the educational program? It has not been my intent to argue that these teachers, and teachers elsewhere, are doing bad work. Quite the contrary. Andy Abraham and Craig Zack, like their colleagues everywhere, wanted very much to provide the best educational experiences to their students.

The conceptual framework I introduced in Chapter 1 proved useful for explaining what transpired. The teachers played an important part in constructing their role expectation. Their activities manifested not only the school district's operational definition of teaching but also their own, indicating the extent to which their work subscribed to educational aims. The teachers' activities and perceptions could have indicated a subscription to an ideal role expectation, but too often their conduct showed them instead to be supporting a negative workplace mentality. They were facing reality instead of the ideal—that is why the negative mentality emerged. Faculty life at Truman High made it very difficult for the teachers themselves to redress their institution's unfair conditions.

How does a school balance out the demand for academic scholarship with that for co-curricular activities? Can or should an individual teacher work in both areas? Each area is an important and necessary aspect of a good high school program. Instead of striving in reasonable ways to resolve this dichotomy, at Truman High the teachers were coping in inappropriate ways. Whether a teacher subscribed to the ethos of Coach or Academic clique, the organization for work in the high school offered little help with their conflict. The teachers perceived that difficulty with the dual-role expectation had less to do with the differences between Academics and Coaches than it had to do with a locus of control that was outside of the teacher subculture.

These teachers had adapted themselves to the conditions for work at their institution. They lacked autonomy and decision-making power in regard to important aspects of their work. Although their opportunities for collegial relations were few, their informal activities were nonetheless evident and effective. However, they lacked collective agreement about what and how to constitute an appropriate idea for workplace conduct. The institution's neglectful tendencies notwithstanding, the teachers' chief internal source of difficulty was their focus on maintenance of normative conduct that was inconsistent with the idealized role of a teacher. They were sustaining a role expectation for teaching that was not quite professional, despite the total group's intention of moving in that direction.

Something about the institution has to change. The rapidly occurring transformation of American society, especially the tendencies toward non-traditional family structures and cultural pluralism, make the school the most important institution for the personal and social development of youth. A school organization is out of step if it is non-adaptive and inflexible, and if it denies professional autonomy to its teachers. Boyer (1988) expresses a strong opinion about the teachers' involvement in decision making:

> Above all, teachers must be full partners in the process. If we fail to give them more authority and a sense of their importance—as well as their responsibilities—we will have failed today's dedicated teachers and be unable to attract a new generation of outstanding young people to serve in the classrooms of the nation. And by that failure, we will have limited tragically the educational possibilities of our children. (p. 3)

Something about the teachers has to change, too. They need to reorganize their workday, reconceptualize the array of services that schools must offer to youth, and play an active part in resolving the tensions from seemingly contradictory features and unworkable demands. Also, teachers must confront the sources of occupational disrepute, because doing so is imperative for achieving teacher craft pride and because the high school students' need for adult exemplars is more urgent than it ever was.

It is typical for both large and small organizations to stagnate over time. Their practices become routinized and their vocabularies undergo little or no substantive change. A stagnant operation is like the common variety of music troupe that entertains its typical audience night after night with worn-out lead lines, jokes, and tunes. In contrast, an improvisational jazz ensemble will explore immediate or uncommon moods and themes, creating innovative variations or entirely new musical expressions. This is the time for teachers to stop doing business as usual and, instead, to explore new ideas for formal and informal aspects of their occupation. In their pursuit of an improved private and public image, they should inquire about self-conscious and unselfconscious teacher mannerisms and about a self-critical perspective on the occupational stereotype. In these ways teachers could break with negative stereotypes and influence directly the advancement of teaching toward a responsible, professional, and highly respected craft status.

The present language that educators use to talk about their work is partly responsible for the problem of the schoolteacher's poor self-image. *Elementary or secondary school* and *higher educa-*

tion, shifting to the *junior high school* or *high school,* assignment to *low-level* courses or *college-prep* courses. From where do these words come? What do they signify? What purpose do they serve beyond designating classes of workers and their work? These words and the practices to which they call attention limit the role expectation of teachers, and the entire profession of teaching, to activities specific to a particular context. A new model for workplace conduct may help teachers to change the way they talk about work: in doing so, they could change what they want to do and what they think of themselves (see Rorty, 1989). An expanding language for the occupation of teaching could break down stagnant beliefs that equate a teacher's work with either demeaning activities or prestigious stereotypes.

The new teachers could have a different agenda for their work and a new perspective on their role in society. They could collaborate with school administrators and school boards to operate a benevolent institution. They could take primary responsibility for developing high schools as centers of inquiry and learning in pursuit of humanitarian interests. Their practice could include a continuous, active role in all decision making in reference to the organization of their workday. Due to the teachers' diligent efforts, their students could not only gain essential knowledge and skill, but also could actively engage in processes of inquiry (e.g., historical, literary, moral, scientific, and so on) and regularly present personal expressions of their ideas and skills through artistic and aesthetic activities.

The new teachers could become regular, equal partners in educational policy making and could assume primary responsibility for the improvement of classroom teaching. Throughout the year, they could collaborate with one another for the ongoing development of the total educational program in their high school. Enrollment criteria and teacher-pupil ratios could respect the characteristics of the students who are served and the purposes that teachers have for instruction. These teachers could assume appropriate responsibility for making decisions about curriculum and instruction, including aspects of scheduling and daily classroom operations, selection of content and materials, evaluation of teachers and students, and the choice and use of methods for teaching. These teachers could establish the criteria for their professional conduct and develop official programs to promote the increase of knowledge and skill among their faculties. Their local teacher organizations could accept their share of responsibility for disciplinary action and nonrenewal for the inadequate or inappropriate practice of colleagues.

These teachers could create an in-house substitute system that is flexible and assures continuity for the instructional program, allowing teachers adequate and meaningful support to deal appropriately with their absence for professional and personal needs. There could be many formal and informal occasions when these teachers could interact with one another and with adults working in other crafts and professions. They could convince school authorities that it is in the best educational interests of children to discontinue hiring practices that emphasize lack of experience and the willingness of teachers to work cheap. Emphasis should be placed on reward and recognition to attract and keep the ambitious, skilled, and innovative teachers.

The new high school teachers could maintain a high profile in relations with parents and guardians, including the education of parents in the proper care of adolescent children. These teachers could assist in coordinating a network of community services for the education, welfare, and protection of these youths. The new teachers could be effective, political activists in reference to all things educational in the community. They could establish partnerships with universities for conducting research on teaching, for continuing professional development, and for proactive recruitment and training of the best teacher interns.

Teachers must gain stature as self-conscious, competent, individual workers. Their informal, voluntary subgroups should serve as vital social organizations that support good practice. The high school must function appropriately as a democratic institution for the educational fulfillment of everyone who comes there to learn. At the present time the discretionary activity of teachers may be so little, so informal, and so private that this call for transforming the occupation may discourage cooperation from even the best veteran teachers. The shift toward professionalism or craftpersonship requires an explanatory framework that not only presents an interpretation but also offers suggestions for improving practice. The conceptual framework that I presented suggests ways for teachers to construct their ideal role expectation in relation to the practical aspects of their craft. It should not be seen as *the* answer, but rather as a tool for theorizing that is interesting for its possibilities in view of the teachers' appropriate and intentional participation in school reform. Its use could facilitate movement in a positive direction, allowing teachers to realize more nearly what they can become.

My research shows teachers having problems with the standard, formal organization of a high school. The response of the social studies teachers at Truman High may be representative of what occurs elsewhere. Mediocre and bad work will go on in a high school, just as it will go on in every other workplace, and it will influence in negative ways the high school teacher's role expectation. However, the best teaching can be recognized and can inform the ideal role expectation every teacher shares, leading to greater self-esteem for the individual and to a compelling, positive public image for teaching. Rorty (1989) advises, wisely I believe, that the aim should be "an expanding repertoire of alternative descriptions rather than The One Right Description" (pp. 39–40). Teachers can and should examine their practice reflectively; and acting upon their craft knowledge, they can create *by themselves* the new and expanding definition of teaching.

References

Arendt, H. 1978. *The Life of the Mind*. New York: Harcourt, Brace, Jovanovich.

Argyris, C., & D. Schön. 1974. *Theory in Practice: Increasing Professional Effectiveness*. San Francisco: Jossey-Bass.

Bell, D. 1976. *The Coming of Post-Industrial Society: A Venture in Social Forecasting*. New York: Basic Books.

Bluestone, I. 1989. What education can learn from industry. *Thresholds in Education* 15 (February): 10–12.

Boyer, E. 1983. *High School: A Report on Secondary Education in America*. New York: Harper & Row.

Boyer, E. 1988. *Teacher Involvement in Decisionmaking: A State-by-State Profile*. A special report prepared by The Carnegie Foundation for the Advancement of Teaching. Princeton, NJ: Princeton University Press.

Cooley, C. 1921. *Social Organization: A Study of the Larger Mind*. New York: Charles Scribner's Sons. (Original work published 1909)

Cooper, M. 1988. Whose culture is it, anyway? In A. Lieberman (Ed.), *Building a Professional Culture in Schools* (pp. 45–54). New York: Teachers College Press.

Counts, G. 1952. *Education and American Civilization*. New York: Teachers College Press.

Cusick, P. 1973. *Inside High School: The Student's World*. New York: Holt, Rinehart & Winston.

Cusick, P. 1981. A study of networks among professional staffs in secondary schools. *Educational Administration Quarterly* 17, no. 3 (Summer): 114–138.

Cusick, P. 1983. *The Egalitarian Ideal and the American High School*. New York: Longman.

Darling-Hammond, L. 1988. Policy and professionalism. In A. Lieberman (Ed.), *Building a Professional Culture in Schools* (pp. 55–77). New York: Teachers College Press.

Dewey, J. 1929. *The Quest for Certainty: A Study of the Relation of Knowledge and Action*. New York: Minton, Balch & Company.

Dewey, J. 1933. *How We Think*. New York: D.C. Heath. Original work published 1909.

Eggleston, E. 1892. *The Schoolmaster in Literature*. New York: American Book Co.

Geertz, C. 1983. *Local Knowledge*. New York: Basic Books.

Goffman, E. 1959. *The Presentation of Self in Everyday Life*. New York: Doubleday/Anchor.

Goodlad, J. 1983. *A Place Called School*. New York: McGraw-Hill.

Gracey, H. 1972. *Curriculum or Craftsmanship: Elementary School Teachers in a Bureaucratic System*. Chicago: University of Chicago Press.

Grant, W., & C. Lind. 1979. *Digest of Education Statistics 1979*. Washington, D.C.: U.S. Government Printing Office.

Herbst, J. 1989. *And Sadly Teach: Teacher Education and Professionalization in American Culture*. Madison, WI: University of Wisconsin Press.

Homans, G. 1950. *The Human Group*. New York: Harcourt, Brace and World.

Homans, G. 1967. *The Nature of Social Science*. New York: Harcourt, Brace and World.

Judge, H. 1988. Afterword. In A. Lieberman (Ed.), *Building a Professional Culture in Schools* (pp. 222–231). New York: Teachers College Press.

Kanter, R. 1977. *Men and Women of the Corporation*. New York: Basic Books.

Kaplan, A. 1964. *The Conduct of Inquiry*. San Francisco: Chandler.

Krug, E. 1972. *The Shaping of the American High School*. Madison: University of Wisconsin Press.

LeMasters, E. 1975. *Blue-Collar Aristocrats: Life-Styles at a Working-Class Tavern*. Madison: University of Wisconsin Press.

Lieberman, A., E. Saxl, & M. Miles. 1988. Teacher leadership: Ideology and practice. In A. Lieberman (Ed.), *Building a Professional Culture in Schools* (pp. 148–166). New York: Teachers College Press.

Lortie, D. 1975. *School Teacher: A Sociological Study*. Chicago: University of Chicago Press.

Maeroff, G. 1988. *The Empowerment of Teachers: Overcoming the Crisis of Confidence*. New York: Teachers College Press.

McLaughlin, M., & S. Yee. 1988. School as a place to have a career. In A. Lieberman (Ed.), *Building a Professional Culture in Schools* (pp. 23–44). New York: Teachers College Press.

McPherson, G. 1972. *Small Town Teacher*. Cambridge, MA: Harvard University Press.

Mead, G. 1938. *Philosophy of the Act*. Edited by Charles W. Morris. 1938. Reprint. Chicago: University of Chicago Press, 1972.

Metz, M. 1978. *Classrooms and Corridors*. Berkeley: University of California Press.

Metz, M. 1984. Faculty culture: A case study. Paper presented at the Annual Meeting of The American Sociological Association in San Antonio, Texas.

Pallas, A. 1988. School climate in American high schools. *Teachers College Record* 89 (Summer): 541–554.

Peshkin, A. 1978. *Growing Up American: Schooling and the Survival of Community.* Chicago: University of Chicago Press.

Popkewitz, T. 1984. *Paradigm and Ideology in Educational Research: The Social Functions of the Intellectual.* New York: Falmer.

Putnam, H. 1989. *The Many Faces of Realism.* LaSalle, IL: Open Court.

Raywid, M. 1989. Institutional democracy in schools. *Thresholds in Education* 15 (February): 13–16.

Rorty, R. 1989. *Contingency, Irony, and Solidarity.* New York: Cambridge University Press.

Schön, D. 1983. *The Reflective Practitioner.* New York: Basic Books.

Schrank, R. 1978. *Ten Thousand Working Days.* Cambridge, MA: MIT Press.

Sizer, T. 1985. *Horace's Compromise: The Dilemma of the American High School.* Boston: Houghton Mifflin.

Smith, L. 1986. *Educational Innovations: Then and Now.* New York: Falmer.

Spindler, G. 1982. *Doing the Ethnography of Schooling: Educational Anthropology in Action.* New York: Holt, Rinehart & Winston.

Spradley, J. 1979. *The Ethnographic Interview.* New York: Holt, Rinehart & Winston.

Sykes, G. 1983. Public policy and the problem of teacher quality. In L. S. Shulman & G. Sykes (Eds.), *Handbook of Teaching and Policy.* New York: Longman.

Taylor, F. 1972. *Scientific Management.* Westport, CT: Greenwood Press.

Terkel, S. 1974. *Working: People Talk About What They Do All Day and How They Feel About What They Do.* New York: Pantheon.

Terkel, S. 1981. *American Dreams: Lost and Found.* New York: Ballantine.

Vidich, A., & S. Lyman. 1985. *American Sociology: Worldly Rejections of Religion and Their Directions.* New Haven: Yale University Press.

Waller, W. 1932. *The Sociology of Teaching.* New York: Wiley.

Weber, M. 1947. *The Theory of Social and Economic Organization.* New York: The Free Press. Original work published in 1922.

Wehlage, G. 1981. The purpose of generalization in field-study research. In T. S. Popkewitz & B. R. Tabachnick (Eds.), *The Study of Schooling: Field Based Methodologies in Educational Research and Evaluation* (pp. 211–226). New York: Praeger.

Whyte, W. 1943. *Street Corner Society: The Social Structure of an Italian Slum.* Chicago: University of Chicago Press.

Wirth, A. 1979. *John Dewey as Educator: His Design for Work in Education (1894–1904).* Huntington, NY: Krieger.

Wirth, A. 1989. Towards a post-industrial intelligence: Gadamer and Dewey as guides. *Thresholds in Education* 15 (February): 6–9.

Index

Absences of teachers, hiring
  substitutes for, 97–98, 127
Academic activities, 48. *See also*
  Subject-matter specialists
  balancing demand for co-curricular
    activities and, 124
  parents on teacher support of,
    20–21, 25, 35
Academics, x, xiv, 22, 32, 34, 102. *See
  also* Subject-matter specialists
  administrators and, 40–41, 52–58
  in attempting to secure department
    control, 52–53, 57
  authority structure of, 39–42, 47
  benefits of membership in, 60
  benign neglect and, 105, 107–110
  built-in escapes of, 93
  classroom territories and, 114,
    120–121
  Coaches avoided by, 42
  Coaches offended by, 52
  Coaches ridiculed by, 44–45, 57–59,
    79, 82–83
  co-curricular activities and, 39, 44,
    51, 55, 58
  coping strategies of, 51–59
  and deadness vs. vitality of teachers,
    74–76
  displays of arrogance by, 80–81, 83
  ethos of, 39, 42, 52–53
  feeling fresh and, 91
  importance of, 4
  on leadership of Coaches, 40
  looting schemes of, 109
  and need for professional growth,
    51, 56
  outlets for self-expression created
    by, 50
  physical description of, 38

professional library takeovers by,
    117, 119–121
  ramming technique of, 107–108
  in relationships with non-
    Academics, 42
  role expectations of, 43
  on routinizing process of teaching,
    65
  scholarly study emphasized by, 48
  secret escapes of, 94, 96–97
  social relations of, 41–43
  social structure of, vii–viii, 39–40
  subject-matter territories and,
    107–110, 120
  on teaching methods of Coaches,
    44–45
  the trap and, 77–83
Activities
  formal, 3, 9–10
  informal, 2–3, 5, 9–10
  invitations to participate in, 5
  mutually supportive, 54–55
Administrators, administrations, xiv,
    12, 121
  Academics and, 40–41, 52–58
  on advantages of teachers living
    within district, 19
  and attempts by Academics to
    secure department control, 57
  attendance taking and, 62
  authority exercised by, 2
  black humor strategy and, 52
  built-in escapes and, 93–94
  class-change times and, 62
  classroom observations by, 26
  classroom territories and, 112–116
  Coaches and, 38–39, 43–44, 47–49
  and Coaches working the shit detail,
    48–49

133

Administrators (*continued*)
co-curricular activities and, 21
and deadness vs. vitality of teachers,
74
escapes and, 86–87, 89–91, 93–97,
99–100
feeling fresh and, 91
informal meetings between teachers
and, 29
in maintaining system upholding
interests of educators and
community, 34
and negative workplace mentalities
in teachers, 3
pimping strategy and, 58–59
playing ball strategy and, 43, 45
playing the game strategy and,
53–57
on preparation periods, 120
in private conferences with teachers,
25–27
and recognizing need for self-
expression in teachers, 50–51
relationships between teachers and,
25–29, 53–57, 126–127
role expectations and, 59
and routinizing teaching, 65–67, 74,
78
rules governing teachers vs.,
115–116
secret escapes and, 94–97
on subject-matter specialists vs.
participants in co-curricular
activities, 24
teachers evaluated by, 25–26,
53–54
on teachers' grievances, 85
teachers living outside Rillton
criticized by, 18–19
on teachers' lunch period
responsibilities, 117
teachers threatened with layoffs by,
23
the trap and, 78
Alternative Paradigms conference,
vii
America (Cooke), 46
Arendt, H., 13
Argyris, C., 7
Arrogance, 80–81, 83

Assemblies
conflicts between Academics and
administrators on, 55–56
escapes at, 93
Attendance taking, 61–62
Audiovisual materials, Coaches'
extensive use of, 44–47

Behavior management, 79–84
Academics' use of arrogance in,
80–81, 83
Coaches' use of roughhousing in,
80–83
Behaviors. *See also* Teacher conduct
formal, 13–14
of groups. *See* Groups, group
behaviors; *specific groups*
self-conscious, 10
of students, 2, 70–72, 79–80
unprofessional, 29–30, 94, 97, 99
unselfconscious, 10
Behaviors, informal, 13–14
character of resistance in, 5
for coping with actual or potential
assignments to lower levels,
23
informal activities and, 3, 5, 9–10
negative influences of, 5
relationship between formal
organization of schooling of
teachers and, xi
sources of, 4
stress relieved by, 5
Bell, D., 7
Benign neglect, xiv, 101–122
classroom territories and, 112–116,
120–121
and gym takeovers by Coaches,
116–121
and professional library takeovers
by Academics, 117, 119–121
subject-matter territories and,
106–112, 120
Black humor, 51–52
Bluestone, I., 11
Boards of education, 2, 13, 85
Boyer, Ernest, 1, 21, 125
Bradford, William, 63
Built-in escapes, xiv, 90, 92–94,
99

Class-change times, 62
"Classroom as a Pedagogical System,
  The," vii
Classroom observations, 26
Classroom protocol, 72
Classroom territories
  benign neglect and, 112–116,
    120–121
  eating lunch and, 114–115
  intrusions on, 114
  and questionable school policies,
    115–116
  as sanctuaries, 115
Cliques, xiv, 37–60. *See also*
    Academics; Coaches; Groups,
    group behaviors
  achievement of status in, 43
  and lecturing and recitation, 68, 83
  membership in, 32
  role expectations and, 38, 43, 59–60
Coaches, x, xiv, 22, 32–34, 53, 84
  Academics' arrogance toward, 80–81
  Academics' avoidance of, 42
  Academics' ridiculing of, 44–45,
    57–59, 79, 82–83
  administrators and, 38–39, 43–44,
    47–49
  and attempts of Academics to secure
    department control, 57
  audiovisual materials used by, 44–47
  authority structure of, 40–43, 48–49
  benefits of membership in, 60
  benign neglect and, 105, 107–110,
    116–121
  built-in escapes of, 93
  classroom territories and, 114,
    120–121
  co-curricular activities and, 41–46,
    48–50, 55, 58, 75–76
  coping strategies of, 43–51
  curriculum and, 41
  and deadness vs. vitality of teachers,
    74–76
  ethos of, 38–39
  feeling fresh and, 91
  gym takeovers by, 116–121
  importance of, 4
  knowing students emphasized by,
    48–49
  on leadership of Academics, 41

  low-level course assignments of,
    47–50
  offensiveness of Academics to, 52
  outlets for self-expression created
    by, 50
  physical description of, 38
  role expectations of, 43
  roughhousing technique of, 80–83
  on routinizing process of teaching, 65
  secret escapes of, 94, 96, 116–121
  social relations of, 42–43
  social structure of, vii–viii, 40
  stonewalling tactics of, 107–109
  subject-matter territories and,
    107–110, 120
  teaching methods of, 44–47, 74–75,
    77
  the trap and, 77–83
Co-curricular activities. *See also*
    Sporting events
  Academics and, 39, 44, 51, 55, 58
  balancing demand for academic
    scholarship with, 124
  Coaches' involvement with, 41–46,
    48–50, 55, 58, 75–76
  and deadness vs. vitality of teachers,
    75–76
  as escapes, 93
  exemption from layoffs of teachers
    participating in, 23–24
  parents on teacher support of,
    20–21, 25, 35
  role expectations and teacher
    involvement with, 20–21, 24–25,
    35
  search for psychic rewards in, 21
Collegiality, 1, 4, 11
  of Academics, 41–42, 54, 56–57
  of Coaches, 46
  huddling and, 46
  for ideas about classroom instruction
    or reinforcement of methods, 26
  in interpreting quality and use of
    guiding ideas in teaching, 10
  opportunities for, 50, 124
  playing the game strategy and, 54,
    56–57
  and routinizing teaching, 10, 27,
    67–68, 76–79, 81
  the trap and, 76–79, 81

Communities. *See* Rillton, USA
Commuting. *See also* Rides home
　between Rillton and Idolville, 18–20
Conferences
　informal, 29
　private, 25–27
Cooke, Alistair, 46
Cooley, C., 39
Cooper, M., 3
Coping strategies. *See specific coping
　strategies*
Corporal punishment, 27
Counts, George, xii, 17
Craft pride, 123
Curriculum, curriculum plans. *See
　also* Subject-matter territories
　activism of chairpersons on behalf
　　of, 32
　antagonism between teachers and
　　administrators on, 28
　benign neglect and, 105, 107–110
　Coaches and, 41
　effect of teachers' workplace
　　mentalities on, xiv
　and interactions between small
　　groups of teachers, 14
　naturalistic model in, vii
　social studies department on, 33
　as subject of discussions during
　　rides home, 63–64
　the trap and, 78
Cusick, Philip, 2, 21, 26, 34, 48–49, 57,
　65, 76–77, 82

Darling-Hammond, L., 99, 106
Deadness versus vitality, 68, 73–76, 84
Department chairpersons, 13, 31–32
Departments. *See* Social studies
　departments
Dewey, John, 7
Distancing, 80–81

Eggleston, E., 2
Escapes, 85–100
　administration disapproval of,
　　94–97
　built-in, xiv, 90, 92–94, 99
　from department meetings, 93
　to feel fresh, 90–92, 98–99
　frequency of, 90

mental health days and, 86–90,
　95
secret. *See* Secret escapes
Ethnographic analyses, 12–13
Evaluations, evaluation process
　classroom observations and, 26
　playing the game strategy and,
　　53–54
　semiannual, 25–26

Feeling fresh, 90–92, 98–99

Geertz, Clifford, 63
Goffman, E., 39, 115
Gracey, H., 17
Grant, W., xi
Groups, group behaviors. *See also*
　　Academics; Cliques; Coaches
　informal, 11
　interactions between, 14
　manifestations of formal and
　　informal behaviors in, 14
　role expectations and, 11, 24–25
　workplace mentalities endemic to,
　　11
Guba, Egon, vii
Guidance personnel, 29–31, 64
　antagonism between teachers and,
　　30–31
　escapes of, 89–90
　responsibilities of, 30
　and routinizing teaching, 67
　types of responses to policies and
　　practices of, 31
Gymnasiums, Coaches' lunch time
　takeovers of, 116–121

Heller, Joseph, 51
Herbst, J., 99
High schools. *See also* Truman High
　School
　number of students enrolled in, 1
　problems associated with working
　　in, xiv, 1–11
Hinkley, John, 52
Homans, George, 6, 12
Homework, 62
Horseplay, 4
How We Think (Dewey), 7
Huddling, xiv, 5, 43, 45–47, 49–50, 81

Idolville, USA
  commuting from, 18–20
  sporting events and, 101–103
In-house substitute teachers, 127
In-service sessions
  escapes at, 93–94
  secret escapes from, 95
  teachers of, xiv
Instructional materials, sharing of,
    109–110
Interviews, 12–13

Job satisfaction, 1
Judge, H., 7

Kanter, R., 1, 84
Kaplan, A., 13
Krug, E., 17

Lecturing and recitation, xiv, 68–73,
    83
  bare-bones outlining in, 69
  and deadness vs. vitality of teachers,
    73
  discussion sessions in, 69–70
  escapes and, 92–93
LeMasters, E., 51
Lieberman, A., 11
Lind, C., xi
Looting schemes, 109
Lortie, D., 2, 21, 33, 67–68, 78, 105
Low-level students, 23, 30–31
  Coaches assigned to classes of, 47–50
  and routinizing teaching, 66–67
Lunch breaks
  in classrooms, 114–115
  collegial relations during, 50
  gym takeovers by Coaches during,
    116–121
  professional library takeovers by
    Academics during, 117, 119–121
Lyman, S., 7

McLaughlin, M., 35
McPherson, Gertrude, 90
Maeroff, G., 2, 21, 67, 71
Mannerisms
  of students, 2
  unselfconscious, 5–6
Mead, George Herbert, 9

Mental health days, 86–90, 95
Metz, Mary, 28
Miles, M., 11
Mutually supportive activities, 54–55

Nation, 75
Natural history perspectives, 12–13

Of Plymouth Plantation (Bradford), 63
Order, maintenance of, conflicts
    between Academics and
    administrators on, 56–57

Pallas, A., 3
Parents, 13
  Academics and, 42
  classroom territories and, 115–116
  Coaches and, 42
  escapes and, 87
  on teachers choosing to live outside
    district, 19
  teachers expecting administration
    support in spite of complaints
    of, 27
  on teachers supporting academic
    and co-curricular activities,
    20–21, 25, 35
Participant observations, 12–13
Peshkin, Alan, 18
Pimping, xi, xiv, 5, 51, 58–59, 79,
    82–83
Playing ball, 43–45, 47, 49–50
Playing the game, 51–57
Popkewitz, T., 7
Preparation periods, administration
    on, 120
Pre-service teachers, xiv–xv
Principals. *See* Administrators,
    administrations
Professional growth, 50–51
  Academics on need for, 51, 56
  in-service sessions for, 93–94
  playing the game strategy and, 56
  and routinizing teaching, 76
Professionalism, 7–8, 10, 29–30, 35–36
  resistance to craft pride and, 123
  of secret escapes, 94, 97, 99
Professional libraries, Academics'
    lunch time takeovers of, 117,
    119–121

Put downs, 54
Putnum, Hillary, 7–8

Ramming technique, 107–108
Raywid, M., 11
Reagan, Ronald, 52
Recitation. *See* Lecturing and
    recitation
Reflective thinking, 7–10, 35, 46
Rest rooms, school policies on, 116
Rides home. *See also* Commuting
    curriculum discussed during, 63–64
    personal or family tragedies
        discussed during, 64–65
    students discussed during, 63–65
    as times for expressing frustrations
        associated with routines of
        teaching, 63–68
Rillton, USA, xiv, 13–24
    Academics and, 39, 42, 53
    chief industry of, 15
    churches and synagogues in, 16
    city government of, 15–16
    Coaches and, 43–45, 48
    and deadness vs. vitality of teachers,
        74
    description of, 14–22, 35
    goods and services in, 15
    role expectations and, 59
    social problems of, 16
    sporting events and, 16–17, 20–21,
        101–103
    teachers at Truman High School
        living in, 16–17, 19, 34
    Teacher's Row of, 17
    transmission to schools of values of,
        17
Rillton Public School District
    budget of, 22, 35
    declining student enrollments in,
        23–24, 35
    formal organization of, 22
    tenure for teachers in, 42
Ritual storytelling, 66–67
Role expectations, 9
    of Academics vs. Coaches, 43
    benign neglect and, 103, 121–122
    cliques and, 38, 43, 59–60
    and deadness vs. vitality of teachers,
        73–74

escapes and, 92, 94
huddling and, 46
ideal, 11, 124
importance of, 38
informal organizations for resolution
    of conflicts in, 11, 24–25
and involvement in co-curricular
    work, 20–21, 24–25, 35
and language used to describe
    teachers' work, 126
and lecturing and recitation, 68, 71,
    73
playing ball strategy and, 45
playing the game strategy and, 53,
    55
and routinizing teaching, 67, 71,
    73–74, 78, 84
secret escapes and, 94
and subject-matter specialists,
    20–21, 24–25, 35
teachers' part in construction of, 124
the trap and, 78
Rorty, R., 10, 126, 128
Roughhousing, 80–83
Routines of teaching, xiv, 61–84, 125
    attendance taking and, 61–62
    cliques on, 65
    colleagues on, 10, 27, 67–68, 76–79,
        81
    deadness vs. vitality in, 68, 73–76, 84
    escapes from. *See* Escapes
    excessive, 6, 62
    justifications for, 72
    lecturing and recitation in. *See*
        Lecturing and recitation
    potential misuse of, 70–72
    ramifications of, 2
    reflective thinking in, 10
    relationship between ideas about
        formal and informal functions
        and performance of, 10
    rides home as times for expressing
        frustrations associated with, 63–
        68
    as self-conscious vs. unselfconscious,
        8
    strategies for coping with, 63
    and student-teacher relationships,
        70–72
    as suitable vs. unsuitable, 8–9

tedium arising from, 2
the trap in, 68, 76–84
uncritical use of, 67–68
unselfconscious, 8, 10, 62
working conditions as sanctions for, 67

Saxl, E., 11
Schön, D., 7, 10
School districts. *See* Rillton Public School District
School reform, xii–xiii, 128
Schools. *See also* Truman High School
aspects of teachers' activities attributable to structure of work at, 2
classroom territories and questionable policies of, 115–116
community values transmitted to, 17
reasons for particular mentalities in, 3, 7
reflections on possible changes for, xv, 123–128
social situations in, xiii, 2
teacher conduct in response to circumstances existing in, 10
working conditions in, xiii–xiv, 1–2
Schrank, R., 45, 51, 54–55, 84
Secret escapes, xi, 90, 92, 94–99
classroom territories and, 114
legal and ethical concerns raised by, 95–96
mental health days as, 95
prearrangement of, 96–97
as unprofessional, 94, 97, 99
uses of gym by Coaches as, 116–121
uses of professional library by Academics as, 117, 119–121
Shaw, George Bernard, xii
Sizer, T., 2, 21
Small Town Teacher (McPherson), 90
Smith, Louis M., viii, 12
Social isolation, 2
Social studies departments, 32–35
bickering over subject-matter territories in, 106–109
cliques of. *See* Academics; Cliques; Coaches
coping strategies through faculty subculture of, 33

on curriculum, 33
dual work role of teachers in, 34
escapes from meetings of, 93
on layoffs, 32–33
playing the game to secure strategic control over, 52–53, 57
reason for study on, x
seating arrangement in meetings of, 43
Spindler, George, 12
Sporting events. *See also* Co-curricular activities
in Rillton, 16–17, 20–21, 101–103
Rillton vs. Idolville in, 101–103
Spradley, James, 13
Stonewalling tactics, 107–109
Storytelling, ritual, 66–67
Students, 13, 59
Academics and, 39, 41–42, 52, 55–57, 80–81
behavior of, 2, 70–72, 79–80
benign neglect and, 103–122
black humor strategy and, 52
and built-in escapes, 92–93
Coaches and, 38, 42, 47–49, 80–83
community values introduced to schools through, 17
and deadness vs. vitality of teachers, 75
declining enrollments of, 23–24, 35
embarrassment of, 6
escapes and, 86–94
feeling fresh and, 91–92
female, 55, 57
guidance counselors' classifications of, 30
huddling on problems related to, 46
and lecturing and recitation, 68–72
low-level. *See* Low-level students
mannerisms, antics, and emotional responses of, 2
number enrolled in high schools, 1
playing the game strategy and, 55–57
and routinizing teaching, 66, 69–72, 75–82
rumors about teachers spread by, 72
subject-matter territories and, 110–111

Students (*continued*)
  as subject of discussions during
    rides home, 63–65
  the trap and, 76–81
Subject-matter presentation
  deadness vs. vitality in, 68, 73–76,
    84
  escapes and, 92
  feeling fresh and, 91
  lecture and recitation in, xiv,
    68–73, 83, 92–93
  the trap in, 68, 76–83
Subject-matter specialists. *See also*
  Academics
  deadness vs. vitality of, 76
  and lecturing and recitation, 68
  perceived lack of recognition and
    reward for, 21, 24
  role expectations and, 20–21, 24–25,
    35
  as vulnerable to being laid off,
    23–24
Subject-matter territories
  benign neglect and, 106–112, 120
  classroom interruptions and,
    110–111
Substitute teachers, 97–98, 127
Sykes, G., 66
Systematic soldiering, 4

Taylor, Frederick, 4–5
Teacher conduct, 12, 84
  characteristics of, 7
  classroom territories and, 114
  collective, 10–11
  coping strategies used in. *See
    specific coping strategies*
  educational aims served by, 7
  escapes and, 97, 99–100
  formal aspects of, 9–10
  informal aspects of, 9–11
  meaning of, 4, 7
  relationship between idea of
    teaching and, 9–10
  relationship between workplace
    mentalities and, 4, 7
  resistance to craft pride and
    professionalism in, 123
  in response to circumstances
    existing in schools, 10

  role expectations for. *See* Role
    expectations
  unprofessional. *See* Professionalism
  unselfconscious mannerisms in
    interpretation of, 5–6
  use of reflective thinking in, 7–10
Teacher look, 6
Teachers, teaching
  antagonism between guidance
    personnel and, 30–31
  certification of, x
  effect of workplace mentalities on,
    xiv
  evaluations of, 25–26, 53–54
  fitness for, xii
  grievances of, 85–86
  informal activities of, 2
  informal meetings between
    administrators and, 29
  interpreting quality of, 10
  language used to describe work of,
    126
  lunch period responsibilities of, 117
  need for self-expression in, 50–51
  occupational images constructed by,
    xiii
  occupational requisites for, x
  from outside of Rillton, 17–19
  poor self-images of, 125–126
  in private conferences with
    administrators, 25–27
  problematic nature of, 9
  reasons for particular mentalities in,
    3, 7
  reflections on possible changes
    among, xv, 123–128
  relationship between formal
    organization of schooling and
    informal behaviors of, xi
  relationships between
    administrators and, 25–29,
    53–57, 126–127
  from Rillton community, 16–17, 19,
    34
  rules governing administrators vs.,
    115–116
  social isolation among, 2
  tendencies toward bickering and
    protecting territory among,
    102–103, 106–122

threatened layoffs of, 23–24,
32–33
in tolerating deviant behavior,
72
unions of, 3, 24
women, x–xi
Teacher's world, 4
Team-teaching approach, 75
Telephones, school policies on, 116
Tenure, 42
Terkel, Studs, 1
Textbooks, Coaches' dependency on,
74–75, 77
Togetherness, spirit of, 54–55
Trap, the, 68, 76–84
Truman High School
physical description of, 23
Rillton community members
teaching at, 16–17, 19, 34
setting of, xiv, 12–36
Truman High School, formal
organization of, 22–35, 128
administration in. *See*
Administrators, administrations
department chairpersons in, 13,
31–32
in facilitating education programs,
34
guidance personnel in. *See* Guidance
personnel
local teachers' union in, 24
social studies department in. *See*
Social studies departments
teacher antagonism toward, 21, 24,
27–29

Truman High School, informal
organization of. *See also* Social
studies departments
for resolution of conflicts in role
expectations, 11, 24–25
teacher antagonism toward, 21–22

unselfconscious mannerisms, 5–6

Vidich, A., 7
Vonnegut, Kurt, Jr., 51

Walker, Decker, vii
Waller, W., 2, 8, 39, 63, 65
Weber, M., 6
Wehlage, Gary, 12
Whyte, W., 39
Wirth, A., 11
Working the shit detail, 43, 47–51
Workplace mentalities, 9
benign neglect and, 105
causes of, 3, 7
escapes and, 99
impact of department chairpersons
on, 31
impact on curriculum of, xiv
meaning of, 4
negative, 3, 11
relationship between conduct of
teaching and, 4, 7
and routinizing teaching, 66
of subgroups of teachers, 11
the trap and, 77

Yee, S., 35

About the Author

Charles E. Bruckerhoff is currently Assistant Professor in the Department of Curriculum and Instruction at the School of Education, University of Connecticut. His research interests are curriculum theory, philosophy of education, and the effects of school policy and organization on the classroom teacher. His studies include the issues and problems of at-risk youth, urban collaboratives, and school reform.